HISTORY OF THE WORLD

Civilizations
of the Middle East

**RAINTREE
STECK-VAUGHN**
L I B R A R Y
A Division of Steck-Vaughn Company

First Steck-Vaughn Edition 1992

This book has been reviewed for accuracy by
William Douglas Burgess, Jr., Dept. of History,
East Tennessee State University, Johnson City, Tennessee.

History of the World by Editoriale Jaca Book s.p.a., Milano. Copyright © 1986
by Editoriale Jaca Book.

English translation copyright © 1989 Raintree Publishers Limited Partnership, a
Division of Steck-Vaughn Company.
Published in the United States by Steck-Vaughn Company.

Translated by Hess-Inglin Translation Service.

    2   3   4   5   6   7   8   9   93   92   91   90

Library of Congress Number: 88-26384

Printed and bound in the United States of America.

Library of Congress Cataloging-in-Publication Data

Civiltà e imperi del Medio Oriente. English.
    Civilizations of the Middle East.

    (History of the World)
    Translation of: Civiltà e imperi del Medio Oriente.
    Includes index.
    Summary: Traces the history of Sumeria, Babylon, Assyria, Israel, Persia,
Greece, and Rome from the Neolithic Age until the spread of Christianity.
    1. Middle East—History—To 622—Juvenile literature.   2. Rome History—
Juvenile literature.   3. Greece—History—To 146 B.C.—Juvenile
literature.   4. Greece—History—146 B.C. — A.D. 323—Juvenile literature.
[1. Middle East—History—To 622.]   I. Raintree
Publishers.   II. Title.   III. Series.
DS62.2.C54   1988   939.4—dc19   88-26384
ISBN 0-8172-3303-2

Cover illustration by Francis Balistreri.

TABLE OF CONTENTS

BLACK SEA

Kizil

Lake Tuz

Menderes

Çatal Hüyük

Hacilar

Mureybet

Halaf

Khabur

Ugarit

Ebla

people of the Amorites

Oronte

Byblos

Mari

MEDITERRANEAN SEA

Uadi-en-Natuf

Jericho

The modern states of the Middle East

BLACK SEA

CASPIAN SEA

Kura

Aras

SOVIET UNION

TURKEY

MEDITERRANEAN
SEA

SYRIA

LEBANON

Tigris

AFGHANISTAN

ISRAEL

IRAQ

IRAN

JORDAN

EGYPT

Euphrates

SAUDI ARABIA

KUWAIT

PAKISTAN

INDIA

Nile

PERSIAN GULF

Indus

QATAR

UNITED ARAB
EMIRATES

OMAN

GULF OF OMAN

4

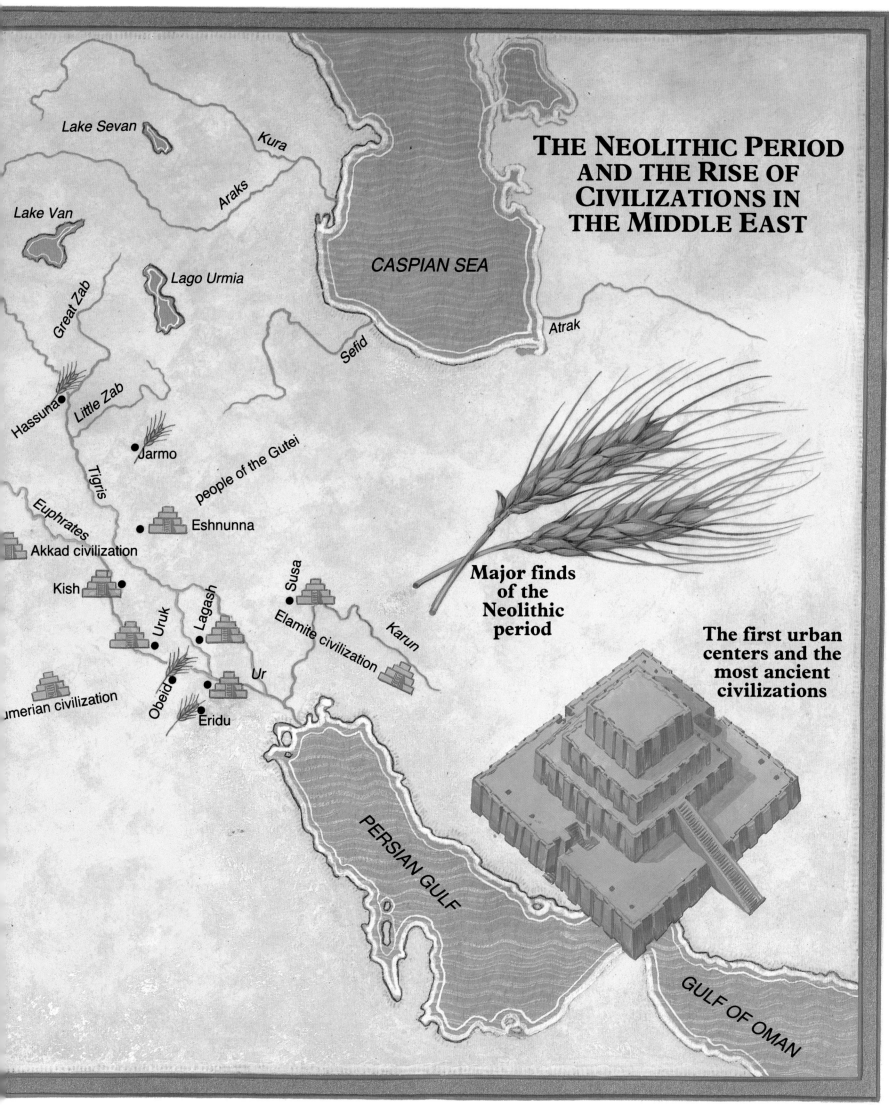

THE NEOLITHIC PERIOD AND THE RISE OF CIVILIZATIONS IN THE MIDDLE EAST

Lake Sevan

Kura

Araks

Lake Van

Lago Urmia

Great Zab

CASPIAN SEA

Sefid

Atrak

Little Zab

Hassuna

Jarmo

Tigris

people of the Gutei

Euphrates

Eshnunna

Akkad civilization

Kish

Susa

Uruk

Lagash

Elamite civilization

Karun

Major finds of the Neolithic period

The first urban centers and the most ancient civilizations

Ur

umerian civilization

Obeid

Eridu

PERSIAN GULF

GULF OF OMAN

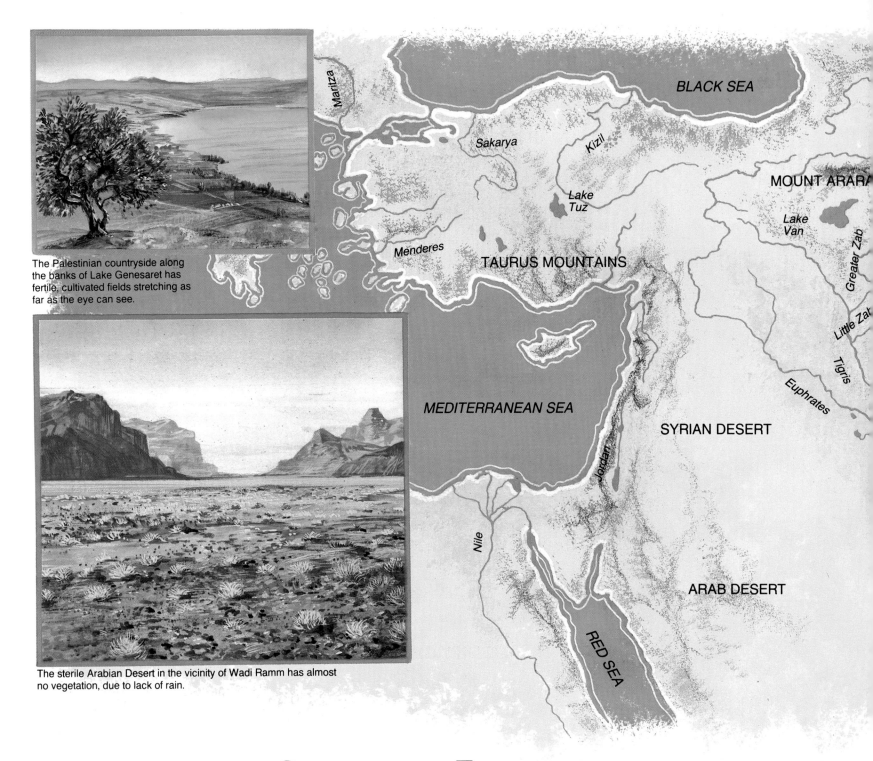

The Palestinian countryside along the banks of Lake Genesaret has fertile, cultivated fields stretching as far as the eye can see.

The sterile Arabian Desert in the vicinity of Wadi Ramm has almost no vegetation, due to lack of rain.

GEOGRAPHIC FEATURES

The Middle East has no exact geographic boundaries. It is a world made up of lands of varying climates and features, with populations showing little similarity to each other. The unity of these lands is due to their geographic position; they form a zone that straddles three continents. They are no longer Europe, nor are they quite Asia. Within them, four major environments can be found: 1) the plateaus and the mountain chains, 2) the Mediterranean regions, 3) the valley between the Tigris and Euphrates rivers, and 4) the desert.

The Plateaus and Mountains

Nearly all of the western territory is an enormous block of high plateaus and mountain ranges. From this rocky barrier, which extends from Mount Ararat in Turkey to Mount Damavand in Iran, the Zagros Mountains run southward. These mountains form a natural border between Iran and Iraq and run along the entire eastern coast of the Persian Gulf. In these regions, winters are extremely cold, and summers are dry. Further, the lines of communication are scarce, and agriculture is difficult.

The Mediterranean Regions

The Mediterranean regions also have mountains of great height. But here, the mountains, once covered with forests, alternate with coastal plains and valleys nestled among the foothills. This is the Levantine Orient: the country of olive oil and wine. Although the climate here has less contrast, nature is more generous, and life is easier.

The Valley Between the Tigris and the Euphrates

The valley of the great rivers bears the Greek name *Mesopotamia*. Despite its dry climate, this vast region is not a desert because of the rivers which run through it: the Tigris (and its tributaries—the Zab, Diyala, and Karun rivers) and the Euphrates (into which the Khabur River flows). Here, agriculture can be rich, but it is tied to the rhythms of the two rivers. Farmers must adjust to a scarce water supply during the dry season. They must adjust again

The banks of the Karun River run along the first spurs of the Zagros Mountains.

Luxurious date palms grow along the bank of the Euphrates River in southern Iraq.

to an excessive supply in spring when the Tigris and the Euphrates overflow their banks and flood the very flat Mesopotamian plain. To deal with this, Mesopotamia's early settlers, the Sumerians, learned to build canals to control the violent floods and to irrigate the terrain. Thus, the Mesopotamian civilization developed because of the rivers but also in spite of them.

Throughout the world, rivers have played an important part in the progress of civilization. Some examples are the Indus River valley, central Soviet Asia (watered by the Amu Darya), and Egypt, which was the site of a very early and brilliant civilization. The plain of Mesopotamia, however, has no wealth of minerals, stones, or wood. Its only plentiful asset is its soil.

Excessive irrigation eventually ruined the rich Mesopotamian soil. Due to insufficient drainage, the lands filled with salt and became sterile. Furthermore, to use land to the south of this valley required such great effort that it, too, was finally abandoned. The remains of the canals, now filled with sand, are barely distinguishable. Today, this region is no longer flooded, thanks to the construction of great dams. Instead, it is the site of an ever-growing desert, inhabited only by a few nomadic tribes.

In the southern part of this area, gently sloping plains have caused the rivers to branch. These branches then rejoin to form a vast delta. This delta is a swampy zone where people have settled for thousands of years. Their settlements

are proof of the human ability to adapt to hostile environments.

The Great Desert

The so-called fertile crescent is the curve that joins the valley of Mesopotamia to the Mediterranean coast and contains the great Syrian-Arabian Desert. The center of the Middle East is a vast, empty, and hostile zone, such as the center of Iran or Turkey. These deserts are interrupted here and there by oases such as those at Damascus, Palmyra, Jericho, and Isfahan. These huge, arid spaces have almost no precipitation.

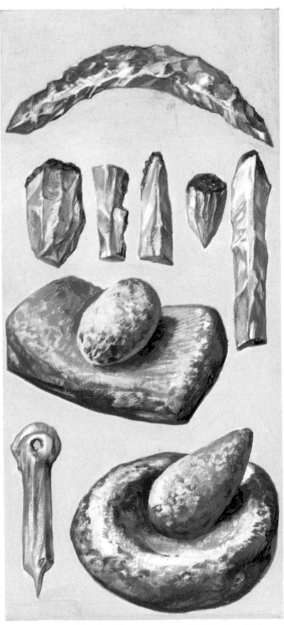

Stone tools, called microliths, were a mark of the Neolithic culture. These tools were found at Jarmo in Iraq: a scythe for grain cultivation, points and blades for various uses, and a mortar and pestle.

In the fields where wheat and barley grew wild, Neolithic people use wooden-handled flint scythes to harvest the plants, which were much smaller and thinner than those of today. Because these grains could be stored, people settled wherever wheat and barley grew. Thus, the first stable settlements appeared. Little by little, people learned to protect the valuable grains against other plants and to save the best kernels for planting the following year. In this way, agriculture was born.

THE REVOLUTION OF THE NEOLITHIC PERIOD

The year 10,000 B.C. marks the beginning of a period of great change in human history. Until this period, humans maintained a hunter-gatherer life-style, strictly tied to the available natural resources. During this period, humans began a farmer-herder life-style and produced their own food. This change was so important to human history, that it is sometimes called the "Neolithic revolution." The most important aspect of this revolution is that the human species learned to act upon the surrounding environment. This ability ensured the greatest possible stability in resources, modified certain vegetable and animal species, and transformed the entire social organization.

The Natufian Period

Everything began in the grassy areas at the foot of the mountains inhabited by little bands of hunter-gatherers. These groups, made up of twenty or thirty people, lived on resources that varied with each new season: fruits, wild cereals, and wild game (especially gazelle). This variety required frequent migrations within a vast territory. These people were known as the Natufian culture and had been named for the locality of Uadi-en-Natuf in Palestine. They occupied the eastern territory from the Nile to the Euphrates between 9000 and 7000 B.C. This period was known as the Natufian period.

Excavations of the Natufian culture have revealed shallow shelters, stone-lined fireplaces, and small pits that may have served as grain bins. These grains were cereals that grew in the surrounding wilderness. Grain had an important advantage over other vegetable products: it could be stored for several months. Because of this, it was no longer necessary to migrate long distances in search of food.

The Discovery of Agriculture and the Rise of Villages

Little by little, Natufian people began to settle wherever wild cereals grew. They learned to recognize the more fruitful varieties and began to plant the kernels from the preceding year to increase their yield. Villages tended to become permanent wherever these food resources were greatest. The simple shelters were gradually replaced by true houses. These houses were round at first but later became rectangular in shape. A new building material appeared: unbaked brick made of mud mixed with straw, roughly shaped by hand.

Pictured above is a reconstruction of a house from 8000 B.C., discovered in the Syrian village of Mureybet. The design is circular, and inside, walls mark off an area for the fireplace, an area for sleeping, and a storage area. The frame of the house is made of wood. The roof and walls are of crude clay, stones, and straw mixed together. Beside the house, a flock of sheep and goats grazes.

In addition to plants, humans domesticated some species of animals. They began with those that lived in groups near the first villages, such as rams, goats, and cows. Little by little, the importance of hunting and the gathering of wild plants diminished. Around 7000 B.C., the main food sources were agriculture and domesticated animals.

Human Settlements Become More Populous

Human settlement was accompanied by a population explosion. This was due, in part, to the fact that migration no longer limited the growth of human groups. As new methods of food production were perfected, single settlements were able to feed populations as large as 150 to 200 people.

Within these communities, however, it was more difficult to settle conflicts than it had been when groups were smaller. Such villages would divide, and a portion of their people would settle elsewhere. Shortly after 7000 B.C., villages began to appear outside the zones where cereals had grown originally. By then, people had learned to cultivate and adapt the grains for new environments. Within a few centuries, this new system of life had spread throughout the fertile regions of the Near East.

In time, the houses were perfected and architecture progressed. Here two masons construct a wall of sun-baked bricks, binding it with clay.

THE BIRTH OF VILLAGES

Toward 6000 B.C., the entire cultivable region of the Near and Middle East was occupied by farmers. They inhabited the zones from which the Neolithic economy had disappeared, but little by little they also settled new territories, especially those upon the great Mesopotamian plain. This period marked the height of a lifestyle in which the village was the basic unit of economic, social, and political activity. In the next two thousand years, inventions were perfected, and new techniques and social relationships were created.

This feminine terra-cotta figurine clasps a baby in her arms. Found at Hacilar, Turkey, this sculpture dates from the recent Neolithic period (6000 B.C.) and perhaps represents a mother-goddess.

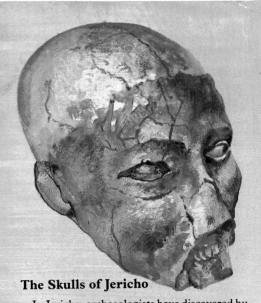

The interior of a sanctuary at Catal Hüyük in Turkey, from approximately 6000 B.C., is pictured. The walls are richly decorated with pictures and animal heads sculpted in gypsum. Many probably represented divinities.

Ceramics

The use of clay vessels, which became widespread before 6000 B.C., was an important change. Before this, vessels had been made of wood, skin, wicker, or stone. However, those of clay provided the ideal means of preserving food. Previously shaped by hand, crockery was soon prepared with more refined techniques. Open-air firing over simple wood fires rapidly gave way to firing in specially constructed furnaces. This permitted potters to obtain and control ever higher temperatures. Like many other objects of daily life, vessels were decorated with painted patterns. Through the evolution of these styles, archaeologists were able to establish various periods. These periods are named after the localities in which their styles dominated: Hassuna (6000-5500 B.C.), Samarra (around 5000 B.C.), Halaf (5500-4750 B.C.), and Obeid (4750-3750 B.C.).

The Discovery of Irrigation

Agriculture and domesticated animals were important in the development of economic life. As plants were cultivated, they changed greatly from their wild forms. The same was true of animals as they were domesticated. With the development of irrigation, cultivation was able to spread even where there was insufficient rain. Thus, the Mesopotamian plain developed.

Village Life

Some villages, such as Hacilar in Turkey or Tell es-Sawan in Iraq, were surrounded by circular walls that may have served as fortifications. Although there may have been armed conflicts, nothing suggests that war was constant. Life was relatively peaceful. Houses in these villages had several rooms, usually grouped around a courtyard. Often the inner walls were decorated with pictures, especially when the

The Skulls of Jericho

In Jericho, archaeologists have discovered human skulls that were removed from their bodies. These skulls, which were specially treated, are also without their lower jaws. The front parts are covered in clay plaster, modeled, and painted to resemble human faces. Shells have been placed where eyes once were. These skulls are from the second phase of the Neolithic period and date back to 7000 B.C. It is not known whether the decoration of skulls indicates an ancestral cult or whether it represents a practice of ancient warrior populations.

The village of Catal Hüyük, reconstructed above, was built on the plateau of Anatolia. Excavations have revealed the existence of more layers. The most ancient date back between 7000 and 6000 B.C.; the most recent date to 5700 B.C. The village was divided into distinct quarters, each of which had its own sanctuary. The houses, built at different levels and positioned back to back with each other, were connected by rooftop terraces. The various terraces were linked by wooden ladders.

The use of ceramic vessels spread throughout the Middle East about 6000 B.C. The top three decorated ceramic vases are from the Hassuna period; the one at the bottom is from the Samarra period.

buildings were used for religious purposes. At Catal Hüyük, in Turkey, frescoes and clay reliefs still cover the sanctuary walls. These works of art reveal the richness of ancient mythology: heads of bulls, sculpted leopards, and hunting scenes with mysterious details.

The dead were buried beneath the houses along with offerings and personal objects. Numerous clay or stone figurines, such as the "mother goddess" of Hacilar, are the only evidence of the ancient religion. Through these objects, historians recognize strong concerns for the earth's fertility, hunting, and the cult of ancestors. Beyond these family observances, it is probable that the population united for collective rituals.

Shortly after 5000 B.C., the first copper objects appeared. This metal had been used in a crude state for quite some time, and sometimes it had been beaten into small utensils and ornaments. But now, the refinement and casting of copper was to benefit from an awareness of the use of heat that had already been applied in furnaces to fire clay. The primitive smiths, like

the potters, became more specialized and traded their products and services for food produced by the farmers. In this way, social relationships

among community members became more complex, and civilizations moved toward the first cities.

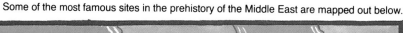

Some of the most famous sites in the prehistory of the Middle East are mapped out below.

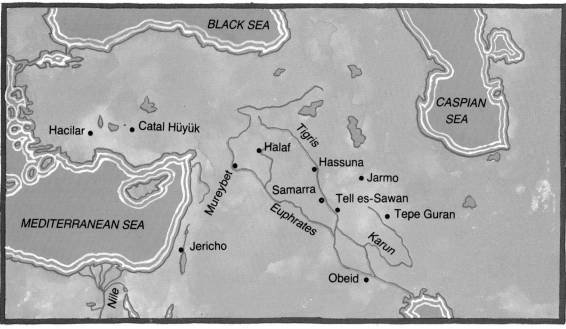

11

Obeidian pottery had detailed, extremely varied decorations. These became less elaborate toward the end of the period. Forms were few, and each corresponded to its practical function.

Clay figures of humans dating from 4000 B.C. were found at Ur and Eridu. The facial features give these sculptures a shape resembling snakes. The bumps upon the chests may represent some kind of personal adornment.

The major sites of the Obeid culture are noted with dots; the region of the Uruk culture is shown in yellow.

The Obeidian village of Gawra is pictured. A potter fashions clay vessels, while other people separate grain from chaff, throwing the grain into the air upon woven mats. In the background a herd of pigs returns from the pasture.

THE OBEID CULTURE

At first sight, the Obeid culture appears unimpressive. But it was here that a long evolutionary process began, culminating two thousand years later with the rise of the Sumerian civilization. This culture lasted throughout the fifth millennium B.C., but very little is actually known about it except its last phases. The Obeid influence reached as far as Syria to the north, but the southern culture emerged as the more innovative, as if the hostile environment had pushed humanity to adopt original solutions.

Means of Subsistence

The earth of southern Mesopotamia is fertile but yields fruit only if it is irrigated. The Obeid civilization was able to expand from the Tigris and Euphrates rivers and colonize the interior only after learning to manipulate water.

With water, cereals could be cultivated. Cereals, as noted earlier, had become important because they could be stored long after the harvest. However, nothing is known of the agricultural techniques that were used. Domesticated animals were important, especially pigs and oxen. In the north, sheep and goats predominated. Fishing was also highly developed in the south.

Pottery

Since their country was poor in raw materi-

Pictured here is a schematic drawing of an Obeid dwelling.

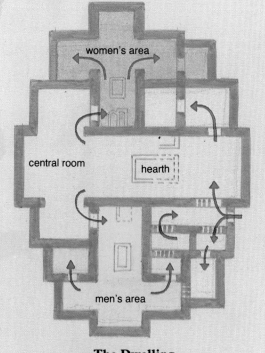

The Dwelling

This private dwelling is reconstructed according to excavations at Kheit Qasim in Hamrin. The plan shows that the house had three distinct sections. The first section included a large space at the farthest distance from the single entrance. This was the most private part of the house, where men and women could find refuge in their own separate quarters. In the diagram, the women's area is shown in pink; the men's area is in green. The second section was a series of connected rooms that were either corridors (such as the entrance atrium and the staircase which led to the roof) or servants' rooms. The great central room, with its central hearth, was situated between the private apartments and the outside. This room was the heart of the house. It served as a welcoming area, as a passageway to the rest of the building, and as a meeting place for all family members, where daily activities took place.

als, the Obeidians were forced to make maximum use of their environmental resources. The best of these was clay. Clay was the best construction material in this area, competing only with reeds.

Clay was also the material used most often in making utensils for everyday life. These objects ranged from handmade ceramics ornamented with geometric patterns to objects used in fishing (scales) or weaving (spindles, loom weights), to tools used to harvest plants (scythes), to ornaments for dress (beads and bangles), to religious objects (figurines). Except for clay, the people of this civilization had very little available to them. They were forced to go elsewhere to find materials that were very rare or nonexistent in their land.

Houses

All of the Obeid villages discovered through archaeological excavations have been found in central or northern Mesopotamia. Each village included a small number of independent dwellings. All of these were built according to a single design, and each was large enough to hold a family of ten people. In contrast, houses in the south (at Eridu, Uruk, and Tell Uqair) were larger and more fully decorated. For many years, these were believed to be temples.

Graves

The only remains which could be connected to religious life are some small statues of animals and human beings. These must have served in ritual magic. Burial customs tell little about the culture. Adults were usually buried in cemeteries near their homes, while the children were buried under the floors of houses. Items also found in graves included urns full of food and drink for the afterlife, and jewelry.

Society

In the Obeid society it seems that work was divided according to sex. Some individuals specialized in a technical field that required an apprenticeship (pottery, flint cutting). Long-distance trade was not yet highly developed, and technology was in its early stages. Luxury objects did not exist, and funeral practices were rather simple, indicating a society that was uncomplicated. The architecture seems to indicate, however, that in the south, around 4000 B.C., a category of privileged people was emerging. These people, through the hoarding of cereals, the control of irrigation networks, and the monopolization of trade, found means to extend their power.

Across top: Pictured is the wall of Habuba-Kabira (Syria). The great Urukian cities were surrounded by walls that served as barriers between a secure society and a hostile world. *Above:* The temple of Tell Uqair, like many important sites, had a great, richly decorated building built on top of a high terrace. These were either temples or the houses of community leaders.

URUK CULTURE: THE BIRTH OF CITIES

The culture of Uruk-Gemdet Nasr (see map in previous chapter) spanned the fourth millennium and was derived from the Obeidian culture of southern Mesopotamia. The most ancient periods of this culture, ancient and middle Uruk, are little understood, but the signs of social change were already apparent. Painted pottery vanished to make way for new undecorated forms. Perhaps painting was considered a waste of time in an economy increasingly concerned with production. But more probably, the disappearance of certain social values was accompanied by the disappearance of those patterns that were their symbols. Burial customs also changed. Some practices, which had

been standard before, gave way to more choices, and burial objects began to reflect the social status of the dead.

Unfortunately, these bits of evidence are scarce. Even when the information available from the ancient periods is compared to evidence from later periods (such as the recent Uruk and Gemdet Nasr), the causes of such change remain indefinite.

The Aristocracy

In this epoch, southern Mesopotamia was broken into small kingdoms, each with at least one city of great size. These cities were protected by walls and governed by aristocratic dynasties. Rich and powerful, this elite class lived in luxury, commissioning finely crafted precious objects from artisans and organizing great banquets. The remains of such occasions have been found in heaps of raw clay pottery, mass-produced for the occasion. This elite

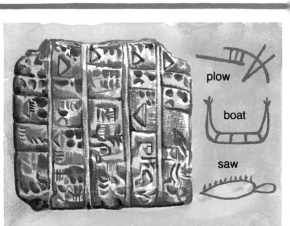

The Alphabet

This ancient clay tablet is from Gemdet Nasr. To support an increasingly complex economy, the Urukians invented a graphic system which allowed for a written record. Simple sales records from about 3000 B.C. are the earliest evidence of this alphabet. The records, however, are understandable only to the workers who kept them. The system was not able to record all the details of the spoken language. Some of the signs scratched into the clay with a stylus are drawings of recognizable objects. Others are figures that undoubtedly are symbolic.

A basalt stele from Uruk shows a lion hunt. The stele dates from between 4000 and 3000 B.C.

Cylindrical clay seals such as this one from Gemdet Nasr were used by Urukian administrators as official signatures.

Above, right: Some seals from about 3000 B.C. reproduce illustrations of reed buildings from the late Urukian period, similar to modern huts of the southern swamps of Iraq. Above, left, is a building in Uruk, the Hall of the Columns. The walls and colonnades of this enormous building were decorated with little cones of tinted clay or stone, arranged in geometric patterns.

group also built luxurious residences. Sometimes, as in Uruk, they built giant complexes combining temples, palaces, and embellished courtyards unlike any previous or since.

The aristocracy controlled all agricultural production (the land, those who farmed it, and the irrigation network) and all long-distance commerce. For the supply of raw materials, which the south lacked, colonies were created in Syria to the north, and fortresses were built to protect the principal trade routes. The elite controlled all systems of distribution, especially those for luxury goods.

Religion and Art

During this time, religion underwent some important changes. Divine personalities became more distinct, and the world of the divinities became organized. The divine world was now a model of the human world. The king became

the gods' representative on earth. It was his responsibility to see that the gods' laws were respected and that order (or culture, symbolized by a walled city) should triumph over chaos (or nature, symbolized by wild beasts, nomads, or foreigners).

This new religious viewpoint also influenced art. What might be called propagandistic art appeared in this epoch. This art, which included three-dimensional sculpture, bas-relief, and glyptic sculpture, depicted the king symbolically assuring the society's security and prosper-ity. The end of the fourth millennium thus saw one of the most innovative ages in Mesopotamian history. In all fields, an enthusiasm for invention was displayed that has never been equaled. With the Sumerian epoch, however, expansionism led to conflict among neighboring cities. For a long time, war absorbed the greater part of the culture's energy.

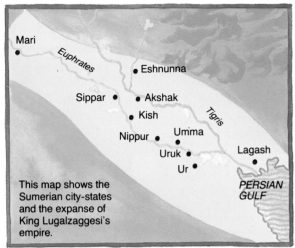

This map shows the Sumerian city-states and the expanse of King Lugalzaggesi's empire.

Two wide-eyed statues are apparently praying. Discovered in the temple of the god Abu, at Eshnunna, they date from between 3000 and 2000 B.C. The eyes are encrusted with semiprecious stones called lapis lazuli. The male statue's short skirt ends in a Kaunakes, the common dress of the Sumerians, made of flaps of fur or sheep's wool.

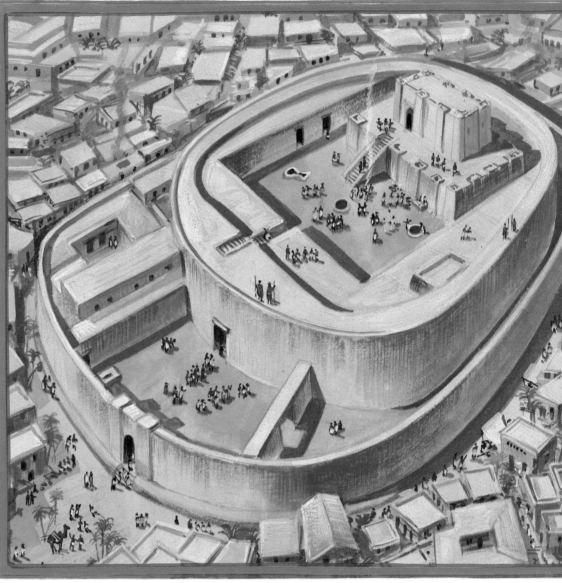

The oval temple of Khafage, the Ancient Tutub, was a huge building which dominated the city. It consisted of three fortified tiers. The lowest level enclosed buildings of the religious cult. The second level contained shops and offices arranged around a courtyard where sacrifices took place. A stairway led to the temple that was erected on the highest level.

THE SUMERIANS

Dynastic Rivalries

The third millennium B.C. is marked by a long series of wars between rival Mesopotamian cities. The more powerful cities, such as Kish, Lagash, Umma, Ur, and Uruk, conquered smaller neighboring cities and became small kingdoms. For some time, the city of Kish was in power. Around 2600 B.C., the power passed on to Ur and Uruk. Even later, power passed to the Lagash dynasty, founded by King Urnanshe. This dynasty reached its height around 2500 B.C. with King Eannatum, who expanded it as far as Mari. Lagash experienced a further glorious period with King Entemena and then declined. Toward 2450 B.C., the reforms of Uru'inimgina, the first Lagash king to concern himself with social justice, weakened the monarchy. The king of Umma, Lugalzaggesi, then easily conquered Lagash, Uruk (which became his capital), Ur, and Kish. He unified the country of the Sumerians for the first time.

Toward 2700 B.C., the title of "lugal" (king) appeared together with the first true palace built apart from the temple. However, the king was still the earthly representative for the god of the city. As civil administrator, he oversaw the functioning of the irrigation network to assure the livelihood of the population. As military administrator, he built fortresses or sent men to war to demonstrate his power. He also undertook the great construction of religious buildings and, in ceremonies, played the role of god.

The cities, spurred by local ambitions, remained fiercely independent. Separated by vast expanses of desert and constantly at war, they did not feel that they belonged to a common civilization. These people also did not realize that they were on the verge of inventing the most precious tool of humanity: writing. Writing was first used for economic purposes, to identify products by various symbols. Later it was used in keeping account books.

Religion

Religious beliefs were another sign that the populations of various cities belonged to a single civilization. Sumerian culture searched for explanations for the world's mysteries, attributing to each divinity a precise function in the universe. Anu was the god of the sky. Enlil was the

A grand funeral procession carries royal dead to the tomb. Courtesans and servants also proceed to their deaths, accompanied by the sound of lyres. These people were often buried with the dead, along with carriages and animals. *Inset:* A golden dagger with its lapis lazuli handle and its decorated sheath comes from the royal tombs of Ur (2500 B.C.). These items give an idea of the objects buried with the kings.

god of air, and Inanna was the feminine divinity. Similar to the mother-goddesses of the Neolithic period, she reigned over the reblossoming of vegetation scorched by the hot summer sun. Gods also personified water, the sun, the moon, war, or wisdom. Each city also honored its own particular god.

The Splendor of the Arts

The Sumerian kings strove to surround themselves with luxury. This desire encouraged an artistic production. For example, the sacred enclosure where the god of the city was worshipped was an imposing structure of many levels. The temple proper was built upon the highest point, to bring humanity closer to divinity. The two great buildings of the temple and the royal palace overshadowed the rest of the city.

The tombs of Ur reveal certain strange Sumerian customs and also the splendid art of their goldsmiths. Kings, queens, and princes were buried in the company of courtesans in festive costume. These people followed the royalty into the afterlife by sacrificing themselves with poison. Members of royalty, ornamented with splendid jewels, were buried along with objects they had used or loved in life. Helmets, weapons, and harnesses were among these items. Highly prized for both jewelry and armor, the combination of gold and lapis lazuli (a semiprecious stone) produced a colorful effect. Mosaics of shells, red limestone, and lapis lazuli came to be used in the decoration of certain objects such as lyres, the most beautiful of which were ornamented with sculpted heads of bulls.

The civilization of the Sumerians attained great prestige before it was conquered by the Semitic King, Sargon I. This occurrence could not have been a violent break from the past since the Semites had been invading Sumerian culture for some time. The result was a fusion of the cultures, guided by the shrewd policy of the new dynasty.

At left: The Banner of Ur (2600 B.C.), a panel with encrustations of mother-of-pearl, with a background of lapis lazuli, illustrates the theme of war and peace. The panel provides information concerning the Sumerian weapons, carriages, and uniforms.

Akkadian conquests were also opportunities for capturing prisoners who could serve as manual laborers. This illustration, based upon a fragment of a stele from Susa, dates from about 2400 B.C.

The bronze head of an Akkadian king was found at Nineveh and has often been identified as Sargon I. More probably it represents his nephew, Naram-Sin. The sophisticated workmanship of the beard and headdress, the severe features, and proud carriage of the monarch reflect the image that he wished to give to the "King of the Universe."

THE AKKADIAN EMPIRE AND THE SUMERIAN REBIRTH

The Akkadian Empire

At the end of the third millennium, the founding of the Akkadian Empire by the Semite Sargon I brought a sudden end to the rivalry among Sumerian cities. Some Semites had long ago abandoned a nomadic life and settled permanently in northern and central Mesopotamia. Some had also settled in the south, where they had mixed with the pre-existing Sumerian population. Due to their numbers, Semites eventually came to govern in place of the Sumerians. After settling in Mesopotamia, the Sumerians had not received any new immigrants from their fatherlands, and they had exhausted their strength in war. The Akkadians transferred political authority from the south to the center of the country, near Kish, in Semitic territory.

An empire of conquerors arose which would come to include all of Mesopotamia and Elam (Susa). It won complete control as far east as the Oman Sea and the Indus River, and as far west as Asia Minor and the Mediterranean. This policy of expansion permitted the empire to obtain—most often by raiding—lumber, stone, metals, and other raw materials absent from Mesopotamia.

Little is known about Sargon I and Naram-Sin, his nephew and one of his successors. Many official records of the empire are lost because Akkad, the capital, has never been found. If the life and successes of this king are founded in legend, it is because he wished to impose upon his subjects a grand, ideal image of the sovereign. With the Akkadian Empire came a completely new concept of power. The rather isolated politics of the Sumerian city-state gave way to an empire which proclaimed itself universal and which glorified royal power. This is reflected in the title attributed to Naram-Sin: "King of Four Quarters of the Earth," which was the Sumerian means of conveying "King of the Universe." In spite of their absolute power, the Akkadians tried to respect the Sumerian culture. The Akkadians themselves already followed many Sumerian traditions, especially religious practices.

Such a huge, diversely populated empire was very vulnerable. Rich and powerful, it was highly desirable. Exhausted by military campaigns, weakened by power struggles, constantly ready to fight rebellions in conquered lands, the empire also had to face invasions of nomadic Semitic populations coming from various sur-

An Enlightened Prince

This statue depicting Gudea, prince of Lagash, is made of rock called diorite. The statue dates from about 2300 B.C. It is among a series of sculptures that represents the high technical quality of Akkadian art. The imperial ideology of the Akkadians is replaced by the image of a humanistic prince, whose face is illuminated by sentiments of piety and wisdom. Lagash had ample means for importing rare and costly materials such as diorite, which most likely came from Oman.

rounding territories. One of these tribes, the Gutans, was responsible for the final fall of the Akkadian Empire around 2200 B.C. After this, the Gutans took control of Mesopotamia.

The Sumerian Rebirth at Lagash and Ur

During the period of disorder that followed, the Sumerian cities recovered their independence and revived. In this time (around 2150 B.C.), the city of Lagash reached a peak in its history with the rise of the prince Gudea. Gudea exerted his influence throughout the entire Sumerian territory as far as Elam. But not until the foundation of the III Dynasty of Ur around 2100 B.C. by King Ur-Nammu, was a true political authority put upon the region.

With this dynasty, the Sumerians again exercised control over the affairs of lower Mesopotamia and of the Ur region (later called Caldea) and conquered a territory at least as large as the Akkadian Empire. This empire, called Neo-Sumerian, lasted a century and made notable accomplishments. In the military field, it revived Mesopotamian unity. The kings of this dynasty, who were great administrators, tried especially to maintain peace. They tried to reorganize and unify the administration, the legal system (the first known list of laws dates from King Ur-Nammu), the religion, and the econ-

omy of the country, and the regions under its authority. The trend toward a central administration that began in the Akkadian epoch now gained full strength. If the Akkadian Empire was military in character, that of the III Dynasty of Ur was the reign of an exacting bureaucracy, which multiplied the number of tablets used in registering, controlling, and keeping accounts. The burden of this empire was to be just as heavy as that of Akkadian imperialism.

It was the Elamites who brought an end to the Sumerian Empire. While nomads flooded in from 1950-1750 B.C., the Elamites infiltrated the nearly overwhelmed Sumerian population and absorbed it. Thus the Sumerians vanished, leaving their language to be used for another two thousand years by scholars and priests. This dead language, which was similar to Latin, remains as proof of the ancient origins of civilization.

The ziggurats were among a group of buildings devoted to the Sumerian cult. This one, of Ur, was built by the Sumerian king Ur-Nammu. It was made of crude brick covered by fired brick, and measured 141 by 207 feet (43 by 63 m) at its base. Three staircases built against the northeastern face met in a portico between the first and second levels. It is possible that the temple on the highest level rested directly upon the second level. Only the lowest level still stands today.

The yellow section on the map depicts the widest expansion of the Akkadian Empire under Naram-Sin.

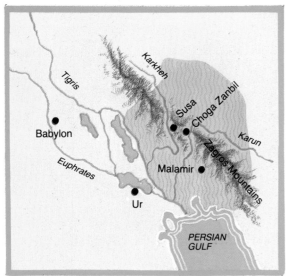

An expanse of the Elamite reign around 1800 B.C. is mapped above.

The plan for the ziggurat at Choga Zanbil is seen here.

One of the principal products of the primitive agricultural Elamite civilization was wheat. It was grown in the plains south of the Karun River. Here farmers gather the wheat to be stored in collective granaries.

A tablet shows Elamite writing.

One of the most expressive works of Elamite art is this head of a man in bronze, dating from around 1500 B.C.

SUSA AND ELAM

The plain of Kuzistan was the agricultural center of the Elamitic country. This region, which is southeast of the Tigris, has a harsh climate and lacks intermediate seasons between the frigid winters and scorching summers. To the west, its communication with Mesopotamia is difficult because of swamps; to the east rises the steep barrier of the Zagros Mountains. Here, by 5000 B.C., a flourishing civilization of villages developed, whose economy was based upon the cultivation of grains. This civilization was closely related to that of Mesopotamia, but the two became great political and military rivals.

Susa, the Capital

The Elamitic society revolved around the capital, Susa. The civilization's economic, political, and religious functions were concentrated

there. Around 3300 B.C., Susa could already be called a city. It had various temples, an army, and an administration that regulated trade. One temple rose from an enormous terrace of raw brick about 33 feet (10 m) high. This structure was similar to those in Mesopotamia at the time, both in form and in its decorations.

In this epoch, Susa's influence extended as far to the east as the border of Afghanistan. It seems that the great city controlled all of the trade with these regions. Susa used this advantage to secure those raw materials (copper and semiprecious stones) that were lacking in its own territory.

Seals and Writing

Seals applied to wet clay were probably the first instruments used by the administration for trade regulation. The seals depicted images of

To the left: A cylindrical seal from Maiolica, dating from 800-700 B.C., was found in the temple of Choga Zanbil. A servant waves a flaglike fan while an enthroned figure, probably a god, lifts a chalice to his lips. *Below:* The imprint from the same seal is partially reproduced.

An Elamite lady of high rank spins cotton on a spindle, while a maid fans her. The palaces of the Elamite nobles often had vaulted roofs, held up by pillars with arches. This illustration is based upon a bas-relief from Susa dating from 1300-1200 B.C.

This terra-cotta vase has painted decorations. The lid is made of a bowl, which can also serve as a receptacle. This piece was made around 2500 B.C.

economic and social life, with many rural scenes in which animals often substitute for people. However, a more powerful system of management was needed, and Elamitic script was born. It was used in business transactions long before it was used on religious texts.

Relations with the Sumerians and the Akkadians

Around 2900 B.C., Susa lost its independence and came under Sumerian control. From the Sumerians, the Elamitic civilization adopted cuneiform writing. However, it did not lose its wealth or its role in international commerce, even when it ceded political power to a city whose name is known only from ancient texts. Around 2350 B.C., the Akkadian king Sargon I took Susa into his empire with an alliance that would be renewed by his successors. No matter by whom it was ruled, Susa never ceased to flourish, even in a politically shaken world. At the start of the second millennium, a new royal branch made Susa a capital again and extended its power all the way to the Iranian plateau.

The Rebirth and Definitive Decline of Elam

The rebirth of Elam took place in the thirteenth century B.C., with a new dynasty whose greatest ruler, Untash Gal, brought Susa to the height of its power. To beautify the city, he built a completely new capital, Dur Untash (today Choga Zanbil), with a great palace which he later transformed into a huge ziggurat. His successors abandoned this capital to establish themselves at Susa.

In the twelfth century B.C., Elam, which had become a military power, conquered Babylon. But toward 1100 B.C., the Babylonian king Nabuchadnezzar I defeated the Elamites. Elam never appeared again as a political force, but its economic prosperity survived. Susa was reborn yet again from its ruins, and the sovereigns of the Achaemenid Empire (550-330 B.C.) made it one of their capitals. But the Elamitic state, which for three thousand years had played the middleman between the Mesopotamian civilizations and the Iranian world, was by now nearly lost.

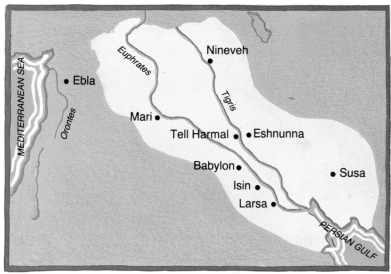

The extent of the Babylonian Empire under Hammurabi is mapped.

To the right: The construction of palaces favored the spread of courtly culture. The sovereigns were entertained by groups of dancers, singers, and musicians that often came from far away. These entertainers were the most precious spoils of war.

HAMMURABI AND THE FIRST BABYLONIAN DYNASTY

For two hundred years after the fall of the III Dynasty of Ur, the balance of power wavered between two cities. They were: Isin in central Mesopotamia, and Larsa in the south (not far from Uruk). These cities, which were heirs to the rival Sumerian city-states, were now in the hands of Amorite dynasties. Both sought control of the small neighboring semitic kingdoms.

The Conquest of Larsa

In 1761 B.C., Larsa was overpowered by Babylonian armies led by Hammurabi, the Amorite chief (1792-1750 B.C.) With this victory, the Babylonians became masters of the entire Sumerian and Akkadian territory, which they renamed Babylonia. The period between 2000 and 1000 B.C., which marked the rise of the city of Babylon, has come to be called the Ancient Babylonian epoch. The origin of the word *Babylon* is unknown. It is neither Sumerian nor Semitic, but the Semites interpreted it as meaning the "door of god."

While the Babylonian kingdom was concentrating its power, other Amorite kingdoms, such as Ebla and Mari, were rising near the "fertile crescent." This whole area eventually became a center of diplomatic and commercial trade. The city of Mari, halfway between Mesopotamia and the Mediterranean Sea, was especially prosperous. Having consolidated his power

in Babylon, Hammurabi reunited Mesopotamia through a series of campaigns directed against the area of the Diyala River, Assyria, and the Middle Euphrates, where he destroyed the powerful Mari of King Zimri-Lim. Though the empire was growing weaker as it expanded, Hammurabi was determined to consolidate a nation. He succeeded in inspiring cooperative behavior in his neighbors rather than dragging his troops through wasteful wars.

The Reign of Hammurabi

As the III Dynasty of Ur had done, Hammurabi attempted to centralize his kingdom's administration. For this, he developed a code of laws, called the Code of Hammurabi. Copies of this collection of laws were sent to all the cities of his kingdom so that it could be universally applied.

From the end of the Akkadian Empire, the economic structure of the country experienced major changes. The state tended to lose some of its rights, while those of the people were increased. Also, in a country where agriculture was the sole means of gaining wealth, land management was not always satisfactory, and it was sometimes necessary to cancel the debts of small farmers. Both of these were signs of social unease and general poverty.

The reign of Hammurabi was characterized

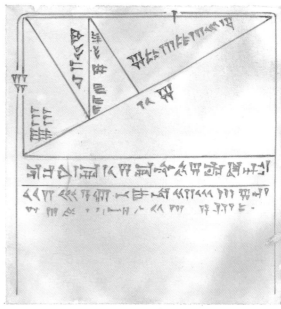

A tablet from Tell Harmal is inscribed with cuneiform writing (an ancient writing form). Here, the mathematician Euclid's work concerning identical triangles is demonstrated.

by the rise of the palace. Every prince built or enlarged his own palace. In the palace of Mari, archaeologists have found some murals that reveal a surprising facet of Mesopotamian art. Schools of scribes were begun outside the palaces and temples, and libraries were built. Here, dictionaries, elaborate mathematical theories, and lists of kings were compiled (marking the beginnings of written history). Tablets containing these texts were found at Tell Harmal, near Baghdad.

Science and Letters

Astronomy was a purely Babylonian inven-

Pictured below is a black basalt stele upon which the Code of Hammurabi is inscribed (from around 1930 B.C.). At the top, the king, who is intermediary between gods and people receives the symbols of power from the god Samas. Between a prologue and epilogue, 282 articles of the law are inscribed. It is the sole copy of the code that has been found whole. It was found at Susa among other Babylonian works taken as spoils of war from the Elamites in the twelfth century.

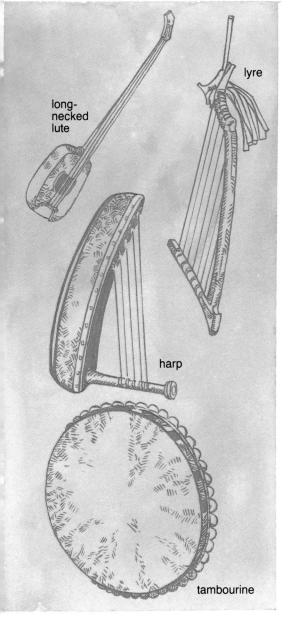

long-necked lute

lyre

harp

tambourine

To left: Among the stringed instruments, the harp played a very important role in the ancient Sumerian civilization. It later returned to fashion during the first dynasty of Babylon in a much smaller form. The box was clasped against the player's body with the strings positioned vertically, horizontally, or at an angle. The long-necked lute was also played. Its strings were plucked, rather than bowed. A variety of percussion instruments including drums, tambourines, and sistrums existed as well.

tion, developed for divination purposes. From the beginning of Hammurabi's reign, the new calendar consisted of lunar months of twenty-nine to thirty days. These months were divided into seven-day weeks which corresponded to the various phases of the moon. The year, which began in spring, was 354 days long. The language of the period was Babylonian, a local adaptation of Akkadian. The most famous literary work of the Mesopotamian past, the *Epic of Gilgamesh*, was written in this epoch.

The Fall of Babylon

For Babylon, as for the kingdoms of Akkad and the III Dynasty of Ur, maintaining such a powerful empire required gifted kings. After Hammurabi's death, all the problems that he had hoped to solve—economic crises and threats from tribes of the Zagros Mountains that had invaded the Mesopotamian plain, particularly the Kassites—brought down the powerful empire. The conquest of the Hittite Mursilis I caused the final fall of Babylon around 1600 B.C. This Hittite conqueror, however, would not be the one to profit from this victory. He left it to the Kassites, who held power from 1600-1150 B.C. but constantly struggled against Hittites and Assyrians.

The procession of Araras, king of the city of Karkemish, is captured in this large bas-relief (760 B.C.).

A terra-cotta vase in the form of a lion dates from about 1900 B.C., Kultepe-Kanish.

A bronze sculpture of a god dating from between 1400 and 1100 B.C. was found near Khattusha, the ancient capital of the Hittite Empire.

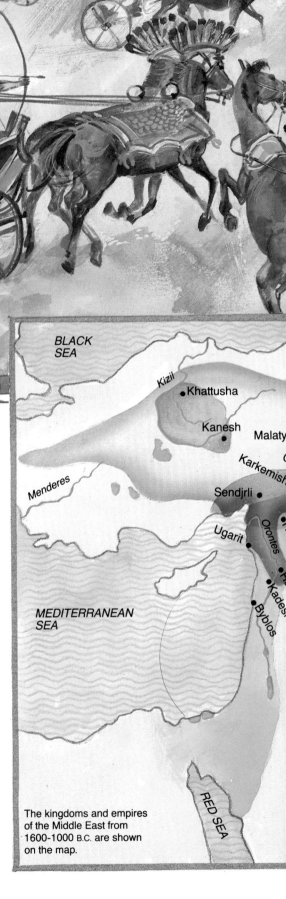

The kingdoms and empires of the Middle East from 1600-1000 B.C. are shown on the map.

HITTITES AND HURRITES

In the end of the third millennium B.C., great changes occurred in Anatolia, the region of the Middle East from which the Neolithic civilization of Catal Hüyük arose and spread. Indo-European people who descended from the Caucasus settled here between 2300 and 2000 B.C. These invaders took the name of Hittites from the inhabitants of the conquered region, which was called Hatti-Hetei.

The Ancient and New Empires

After centuries of slow integration among the newly arrived peoples and their predecessors, the Ancient Empire was born around 1860 B.C. and lasted until 1500 B.C. The first great ruler was Anita, who destroyed the ancient capital of Khattusha and built a new capital at Bogazköy. The period of great expansion had its start with the reign of King Labarna (around 1680 B.C.), which was followed by nearly a century of con-

quests. The army pushed as far as Halpa (Aleppo) in Syria in 1620 B.C. and sacked Babylon in the reign of King Mursilis I, 1595 B.C.

After King Telepinu (1525-1500 B.C.), the empire experienced a century of decline. The second great period of Hittite civilization, known today as the New Empire, began with King Suppiluliuma I in 1380 B.C. Its expansion reached as far southwest as the Aegean Sea. To the southeast, the Hittites defeated the Hurrites under the rule of Mittani.

The new Hittite Empire and the new Egyptian Empire were for some time the two great powers that controlled life in these regions. The Hittites blocked Egyptian advances toward the Euphrates, and with King Muwatallis II (1315-1290 B.C.), defeated the Egyptian army at Kadesh. After this battle, the Hittites slowly declined in the face of rising Assyrian power to the east and the arrival of the "Sea People" from

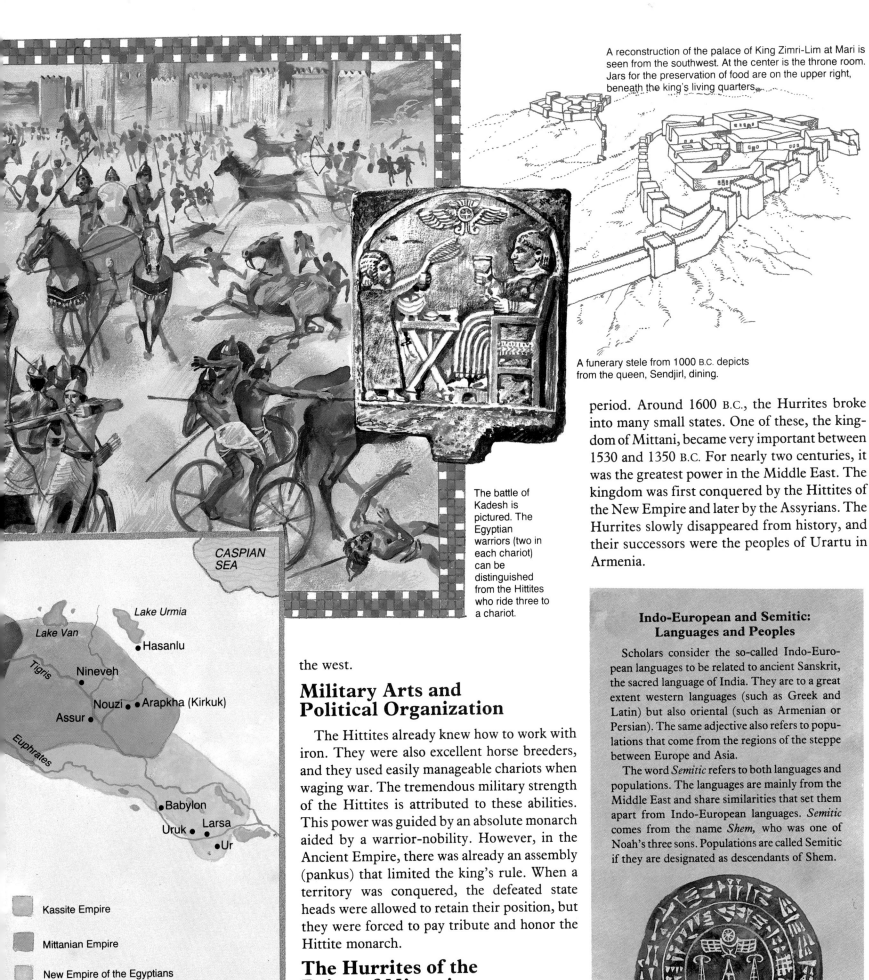

A reconstruction of the palace of King Zimri-Lim at Mari is seen from the southwest. At the center is the throne room. Jars for the preservation of food are on the upper right, beneath the king's living quarters.

A funerary stele from 1000 B.C. depicts from the queen, Sendjirl, dining.

The battle of Kadesh is pictured. The Egyptian warriors (two in each chariot) can be distinguished from the Hittites who ride three to a chariot.

CASPIAN SEA

Lake Urmia

Lake Van

Tigris

● Hasanlu

Nineveh ●

Nouzi ● ● Arapkha (Kirkuk)

Assur ●

Euphrates

● Babylon

Uruk ● Larsa ●

● Ur

Kassite Empire

Mittanian Empire

New Empire of the Egyptians

Ancient Hittite Empire (around 1500 B.C.)

New Hittite Empire at the height of its expansion (around 1300 B.C.)

period. Around 1600 B.C., the Hurrites broke into many small states. One of these, the kingdom of Mittani, became very important between 1530 and 1350 B.C. For nearly two centuries, it was the greatest power in the Middle East. The kingdom was first conquered by the Hittites of the New Empire and later by the Assyrians. The Hurrites slowly disappeared from history, and their successors were the peoples of Urartu in Armenia.

the west.

Military Arts and Political Organization

The Hittites already knew how to work with iron. They were also excellent horse breeders, and they used easily manageable chariots when waging war. The tremendous military strength of the Hittites is attributed to these abilities. This power was guided by an absolute monarch aided by a warrior-nobility. However, in the Ancient Empire, there was already an assembly (pankus) that limited the king's rule. When a territory was conquered, the defeated state heads were allowed to retain their position, but they were forced to pay tribute and honor the Hittite monarch.

The Hurrites of the Reign of Mittani

The Hurrites originated in the southern Caucasus (Armenia-Azerbaijan). These warlike people conquered the regions of the fertile crescent between 3000 and 1000 B.C. They were one of the most important and liveliest cultures of the

Indo-European and Semitic: Languages and Peoples

Scholars consider the so-called Indo-European languages to be related to ancient Sanskrit, the sacred language of India. They are to a great extent western languages (such as Greek and Latin) but also oriental (such as Armenian or Persian). The same adjective also refers to populations that come from the regions of the steppe between Europe and Asia.

The word *Semitic* refers to both languages and populations. The languages are mainly from the Middle East and share similarities that set them apart from Indo-European languages. *Semitic* comes from the name *Shem*, who was one of Noah's three sons. Populations are called Semitic if they are designated as descendants of Shem.

The symbol of the winged sun

This reconstruction is of one of the palaces near Khattusha during the twelfth century B.C.

Officers are at work in one of the archive rooms of the palace at Ebla. The tablets can be seen upon the shelves.

An ancient tablet from Mari contains a list of distributed rations.

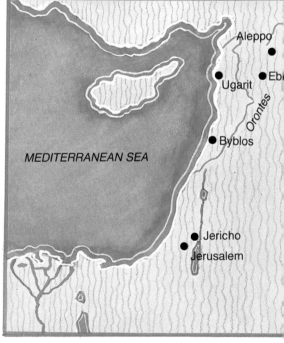

The region of the four cities lies between the Mediterranean and the basin of the Tigris and Euphrates rivers.

CITIES AMONG THE EMPIRES: MARI, EBLA, UGARIT, BYBLOS

The cities of Mari, Ebla, Ugarit, and Byblos were sometimes independent kingdoms and sometimes possessions of an empire. These cities had an important role in the trade between the Mediterranean and the Orient. They also influenced the development of literature, with the contribution of two Semitic languages and the invention of an alphabet. As use of this alphabet spread, cuneiform writing, which had been dominant before this, was eventually abandoned.

Mari, Ford of the Middle Euphrates

Situated at the middle reaches of the Euphrates River, Mari was an important stop between the Mediterranean Sea and the Persian Gulf, or Syria and Babylon. Mari became a cultural center which contributed to the westward spread of writing and art. After two centuries, during which Babylonian influence was extremely strong even in the area of language and literature, the Assyrians of the Ancient Empire conquered the city around 1800 B.C. Around 1775 B.C., King Zimri-Lim, a descendant of the dynasty which had originally ruled Mari, regained the city. For about fifteen years, Mari again became the center of a kingdom which stretched through the middle Euphrates region. The city was eventually destroyed by Hammurabi in 1760 B.C.

Ebla, in the Heart of Syria

Closely tied to Mari by commercial and administrative bonds was the city of Ebla in northern Syria. The site of Ebla was found in 1968 near Tell Mardikh, 70 miles (112 km) south of Aleppo. The city's archives, discovered in 1975, include about sixteen thousand well-preserved clay tablets. The first urban settlement of this kingdom developed in the third millennium B.C. It was repeatedly destroyed and rebuilt for the next thousand years, attaining its greatest splendor between 2400 and 2000 B.C. A great commercial center for animal stock, fabrics, precious stones, and metals, Ebla established relations with many other kingdoms in its time. It was also an extraordinary cultural cen-

Byblos, the great Phoenician commercial city, is viewed from the sea. *In the inset:* Phoenician ships, such as that in the drawing, were used to transport lumber.

center for communications across land and sea. From around 1800 B.C. on, Ugarit was alternately dependent upon Egypt or Mesopotamia with only brief periods of independence. The last two centuries in its history are well known through the city's archives and also from Egyptian archives. Between 1210 and 1195 B.C., Ugarit was destroyed forever, perhaps by an earthquake in combination with invasions of the Sea People.

Byblos, an Ancient Phoenician Center

Byblos is the Greek name of one of the most ancient centers of Phoenician civilization. Its urban development was significant in very early times. From around 2700 B.C., it was alternately dependent upon Egypt and Mesopotamia, and it held great commercial importance. Throughout ancient times, Byblos was coveted by all great powers because of its wealth. Much of this wealth came from the city's commerce in papyrus (or byblos in Greek). In addition to papyrus production, Byblos's economy revolved around fabric production, forestry, and maritime communications. The city was also known for its extremely skilled artisans who did work in gold and ivory. At Byblos, the alphabetical script of Ugarit lost its cuneiform characteristics and acquired those of true writing.

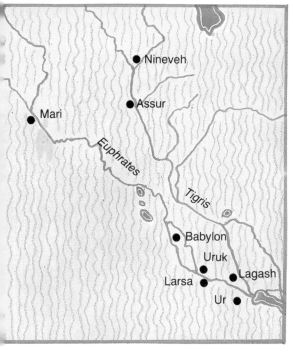

ter, as the abundance of administrative, historical, geographic, and literary texts proves.

Ugarit, the Harbor City

Around 7000 B.C., Ugarit was the most important city in northern Syria and was already engaged in commercial relations with Mesopotamia. It later fell into a decline for nearly two thousand years. Finally, between 2000 and 1000 B.C., it rose again as an important commercial

An ivory sculpture from Ugarit (1400 B.C.) depicts the goddess of fertility.

THE PHOENICIANS IN SYRIA AND PALESTINE

The name *Phoenician* comes from the Greek word *phoinix,* meaning "red-purple." The Greeks named this people for the purple dye used in the fabrics they produced. According to the most ancient historical texts, the Phoenicians called themselves *Canaanites,* a Semitic word meaning "land of purple."

The borders of the Phoenician territory were determined by the Mediterranean Sea to the west. To the east were the mountains of Lebanon and northern Palestine. The geography of the land influenced the Phoenicians in three important ways. First, it separated them from the populations who lived in the interior regions beyond the mountains. Second, the broken coastline kept the Phoenicians from becoming a single political body. It encouraged instead the growth of small city-states. Finally, it pushed the Phoenicians toward the Mediterranean, which was the only territory open to their expansion. Here, they extended their domain with many colonies.

The history of the Phoenicians began around the thirteenth century B.C. At the time, the Mediterranean coast was a region of great change due to the movement of warlike populations called Sea People. Mycenae, the Greek town and commercial empire in the eastern Mediterranean, most likely also fell as a consequence of these events. The Phoenicians took advantage of the situation by seizing their independence. Within a short time, they developed their own trade network.

It is difficult to trace Phoenician activities since they left behind very few direct sources of information. What is known of them has come from the historical documents of other peoples. The history of the Phoenicians, or Canaanites, was always interwoven with that of the Hebrews. Numerous modern archaeological discoveries made of the ancient Phoenician colonies are the sole direct source of information about their architecture, art, religion, and trade. Around 1100 B.C., the Assyrians began to raid the Phoenician territory, and even the Egyptians would invade Phoenician towns to seize needed lumber.

Colonies and Commerce

The first independent colonies were established along the coasts of Spain (Cádiz) and Morocco about 1100 B.C. For the next 250 years, the Phoenicians experienced great prosperity. New towns were founded on the western coast of Spain, on the eastern coast of France, and on the islands of Sardinia, Sicily, Malta, Gozo, and Pantelleria. The most famous and wealthy Phoenician colony was Carthage, which soon became a center of Phoenician culture in the

western Mediterranean. The Phoenicians did a great deal of trading of their agricultural products (oil, wheat, barley, and raisins) and of their craft items (vases, statues, and ivory carvings). But the most sought-after trade item was lumber from the mountain forests. The Phoenicians also traded artifacts and goods that they obtained from other Mediterranean cultures.

The Greek historian and geographer Herodotus wrote of the interesting way in which the Phoenicians traded with the peoples of the African coast. The Phoenicians would arrange their goods on the shore and go back to their ships where they would light a smoky fire. The smoke

A stele with the god Baal on a lion, Amrit, fifth century B.C., is pictured.

attracted the Africans, who would come to the shore, examine the goods, deposit a certain amount of gold beside them, and retreat. The Phoenicians then would go back to shore and evaluate the offer. If the offer was not high enough, they would return to their ships and wait for a higher offer. Trade continued until both sides were satisfied.

The Spread of the Alphabet

One of the major contributions of the Phoe-

nicians was their alphabet, which spread throughout the Mediterranean region. It was the Phoenicians who taught writing with an alphabet to the Greeks, and both populations later spread its knowledge.

The Religion

The Phoenicians had a polytheistic religion, which means they honored many gods. The main gods were El-Elat and Baal-Baalat. El was called "the Beaming," while Baal was referred to as "the Lord." Baal was more ordinary and more active than El. He was the sovereign, the warrior, the principle of fertility, and the crea-

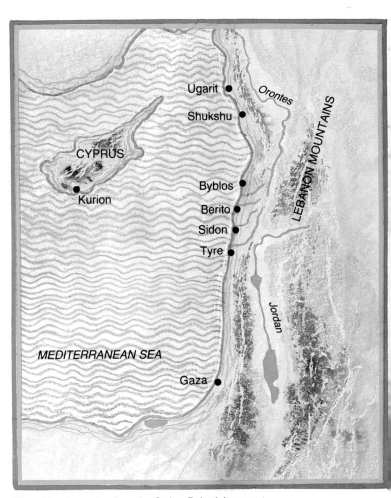

Phoenician towns lie along the Syrian-Palestinian coast.

tor of the world. Each town had its own particular deities.

Modern excavations have brought to light sacrificial sites, which are called tofets. Children or small animals were sacrificed at these sites. So far, such sacrificial sites have been found only in the western Phoenician colonies of Carthage, Souse (Hadrumetum), Motia (in Sicily), Sulcis, and Tharsos (in Sardinia).

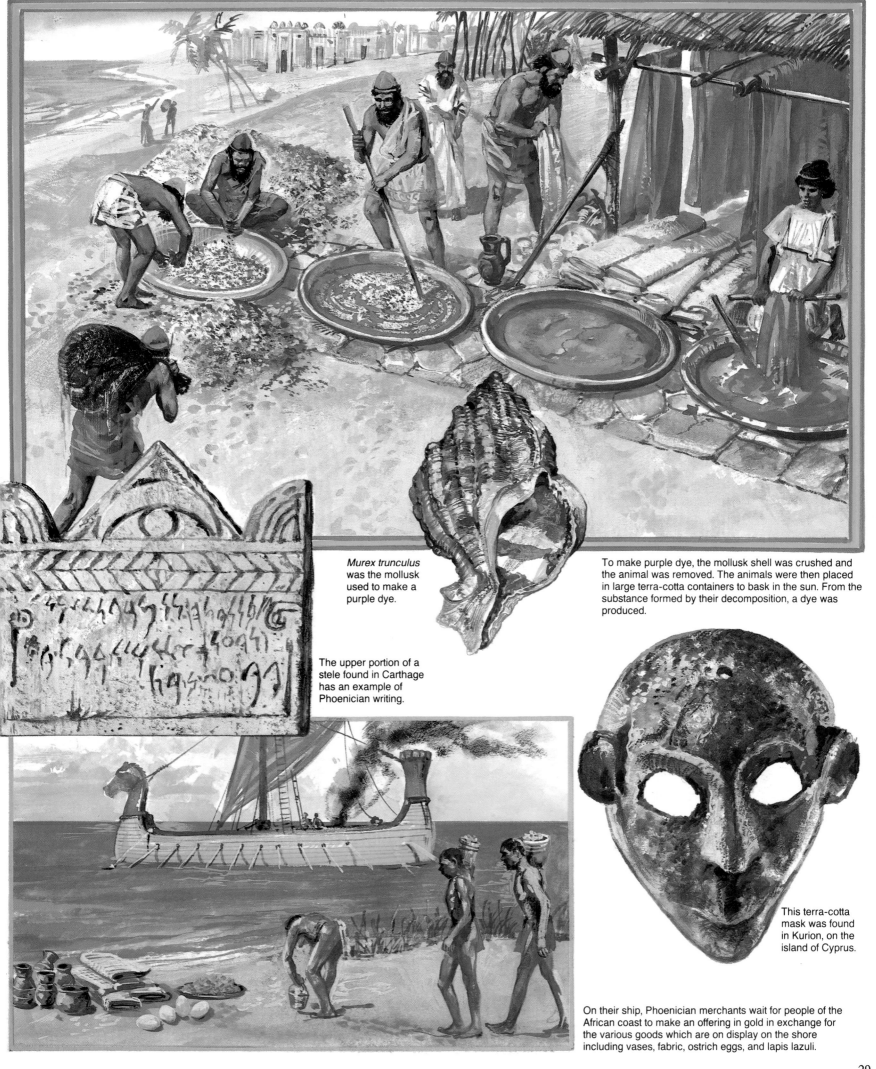

Murex trunculus was the mollusk used to make a purple dye.

To make purple dye, the mollusk shell was crushed and the animal was removed. The animals were then placed in large terra-cotta containers to bask in the sun. From the substance formed by their decomposition, a dye was produced.

The upper portion of a stele found in Carthage has an example of Phoenician writing.

This terra-cotta mask was found in Kurion, on the island of Cyprus.

On their ship, Phoenician merchants wait for people of the African coast to make an offering in gold in exchange for the various goods which are on display on the shore including vases, fabric, ostrich eggs, and lapis lazuli.

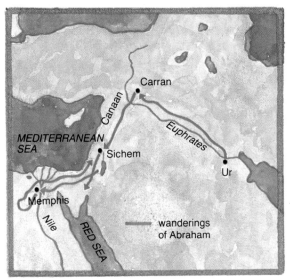

Abraham's journey from Ur to Canaan to Egypt and back to Canaan is marked in green.

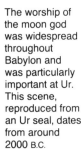

The worship of the moon god was widespread throughout Babylon and was particularly important at Ur. This scene, reproduced from an Ur seal, dates from around 2000 B.C.

During the age of the patriarchs, one tribe rests at an oasis as another caravan that has just crossed the desert arrives.

ancient paths across the Sinai Peninsula

Part of the stele that celebrates the victory of Pharaoh Merneptah (around 1200 B.C.) is seen here. The word *Israel* carved in it is the earliest known mention of the name.

ISRAEL FROM ABRAHAM TO THE JUDGES

Abraham and the Birth of the Hebrew People

According to the Bible, Abraham, the founder of the Hebrew people, lived around 1850 B.C. Abraham was a shepherd and a descendant of Shem, one of Noah's three sons. He was the "father of all of the sons of Eber" of the family of Terah, and lived in the Sumerian town of Ur. Most likely, after the fall of the III Dynasty of Ur, Abraham and his relatives were forced to abandon their homeland. From there they traveled along the course of the Euphrates until they reached Haran. This migration through the Paddan Aram (or the Plain of Aram) is very important in biblical history. The movement of these people is recorded in historical documents of the populations who lived in that region (Hittites and Hurrites).

The Arrival in Canaan and the First Ancestors

Guided by a divine promise, Abraham made his way to the land of Canaan, with his wife Sarah and his nephew Lot. He led a seminomadic life, and stopped for a while in the southern areas close to the Negheb, which was sparsely populated and had no towns. The route of his wanderings is dotted with sacred sites, such as Sichem.

Abraham had two sons: Ismael, who was considered the ancestor of the Arabic people, and Isaac. Ismael married in the land of Canaan, while Isaac chose a wife for himself from among his people in Haran. Isaac also had two sons, Esau and Jacob. Jacob, who was also called Israel, had twelve sons. These twelve sons are credited with forming the Twelve Tribes of Israel, or the Israelites, to which the Hebrews trace their ancestors.

The Sojourn in Egypt and the Exodus

When famine struck the land of Canaan, one of Jacob's sons, Joseph, led the Israelites to Egypt. There they settled in a region suitable for sheep herding and were successful. Soon they had attained much wealth and prestige like Jacob before them. This prosperous period in

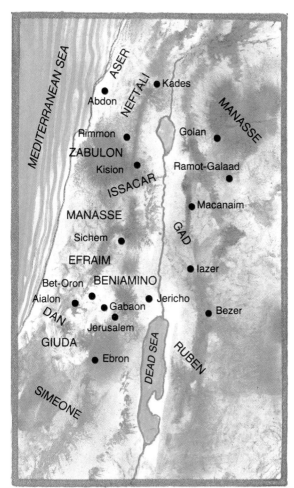

The paths that crossed the desert in the time of the Hebrew Exodus from Egypt are mapped. The triangles represent the various locations for Mount Sinai as proposed by scholars.

A serpent mounted on a pole symbolizes the permanence of the Hebrew people in the desert. The Bible says that Moses protected his people against the threat of poisonous snakes by raising a bronze serpent, according to God's command.

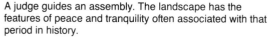

A judge guides an assembly. The landscape has the features of peace and tranquility often associated with that period in history.

The Promised Land and the Twelve Tribes of Israel are shown.

A three-legged mortar was found at Hazor. It dates from the period immediately following the Epoch of the Judges, although certain similar objects also existed before that date.

Egypt lasted only two hundred years, until the period of Egyptian revolt under the reigns of Ramses II (1298-1232 B.C.) and his successor Merneptah (1232-1224 B.C.). With the new pharaoh, the Israelites lost their social positions and many were forced into slavery. The Israelites remained slaves until Moses led them from Egypt in 1200 B.C. This flight from Egypt, called Exodus, is the epic at the heart of Hebrew history and religion. The incident includes important events such as the plagues of Egypt, the feast of Passover, the miraculous escape, the presence of God upon Mount Sinai, the law of the Ten Commandments, the pilgrimage through the desert before reaching Canaan, and the Promised Land.

The Return to Canaan: The Age of the Judges

Moses died before he and his people reached Canaan. However, under the direction of Moses' successor, Joshua, the Hebrews crossed the River Jordan in the region of Jericho and settled in Canaan. This was a slow and difficult process that would last almost two hundred years. During this time, the Israelites were constantly at war with local populations such as the Canaanites and the Philistines. But Hebrew culture was almost completely unprepared for war. This and the division of the Hebrews into twelve tribes made their armies weaker than those of the local populations.

In time, charismatic leaders, called judges, arose. A judge's influence was limited to one tribe and to local events. Eventually the tribes realized the need for a central government. They turned to Samuel, a judge who was respected by the majority of the Hebrew people, and asked him to appoint a king. Around 1020 B.C., Samuel appointed Saul as the first Hebrew king.

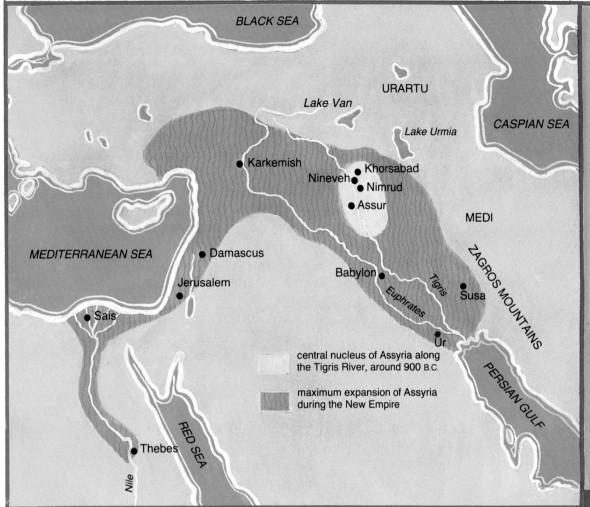

The Assyrian Empire is pictured above.

THE ASSYRIAN EMPIRE

The Assyrians were a part of the very ancient immigration of Semitic people, known as the Amorites. The immigration occurred throughout the region of Mesopotamia around the twentieth century B.C. The Assyrians settled the northern part of Mesopotamia, south of Lake Van and of the Armenian border, and west of the Zagros Mountains. To the south, their territory bordered the Babylonian kingdom.

The Ancient Empire

The history of the Assyrians begins at the end of the III Dynasty of Ur. This dynasty lost its power to the Amorite leaders of Assur, Babylon, and Mari around 1950 B.C. The Ancient Empire (1950-1365 B.C.) was a long period marked by a movement away from farming. During this time, trade became important and a large trade network developed, stretching primarily westward toward Anatolia. The Assyrians established colonies at important crossroads along the trade routes. This promising beginning for the Assyrians was interrupted by hostile invasions. At first they were defeated by Hammurabi, the king of Babylon. Later they were forced to surrender to the Hurrites

The Middle Empire

The Middle Empire (1365-932 B.C.) was a period of Assyrian power, marked by the formation of a great empire. To the west, the Assyrians pushed as far as the Mediterranean, and to the southeast they conquered all of southern Mesopotamia. The empire became increasingly rich, both economically and culturally. Economically, the fertility of the southern plain and the plentiful western forests were wealthy resources. Culturally, the empire advanced mainly through contact with the Babylonian and Sumerian cultures, both of which were more advanced. The Assyrian civilization came to be a great influence in the evolution of the ancient Middle East.

The New Empire

The New Empire (932-612 B.C.) marked the peak of Assyrian power. The army was strengthened by the addition of a cavalry which admit-

The Assyrian military camps were highly organized. Here, an officer's tent stands in the middle of the camp. Camels, seen in the background, were used for the first time in the epoch of Ashurbanipal.

In the throne room of Nimrud, King Ashurnasirpal II (seated) meets with a dignitary. This king reigned from 883-859 B.C.

ted only members of the upper class and with the addition of an infantry made up of various classes. The monarchy continued to pursue the dream of a universal empire.

In this period, the Assyrians earned their reputation as cruel and bloodthirsty warriors. They abused the resources of conquered peoples, increasing their own wealth and well-being, and inspired terror in all populations near and far. The Assyrian army swarmed over the regions of Babylon, Urartu, Phoenicia, Syria, Palestine, Elam, and Egypt.

The Assyrian king Tiglath-pileser III (745-727 B.C.) changed the shape of the whole eastern world. Under this ferocious and merciless king, Assyria became a tremendously powerful force. To better control conquered populations, he would uproot the people of one country and transport them to another region. He also divided his empire into provinces that were governed by his own military officers. King Ashurbanipal (668-626 B.C.) concluded the campaigns against Egypt. After his death, Assyria began to decline. In 612 B.C. the Medes, with the Babylonians, invaded Assyria and destroyed Nineveh. After 609 B.C., the Assyrians vanished.

The inscriptions below, written by the Assyrian kings, describe their wars and victories:

From the *Prism* of King Sennacherib

"Hezekiah of Judah did not want to put himself beneath my yoke. I besieged forty-six of his forty-five towns and innumerable small villages nearby. I conquered them, building embankments, erecting towers, and pushing these close to the walls with assault troops . . . I looted the towns and deported, as prisoners, 200,150 people. . . . I imprisoned him (Hezekiah) in his residence in Jerusalem, like a bird in a cage. . . ."

From the *Annals* of Shalmaneser III (858-824 B.C.)

"In the eighteenth year of my reign, I crossed the Euphrates River for the sixteenth time. Azael, King of Damascus, trusting the strength of his army, gathered a great number of soldiers. . . . Fighting against him I inflicted a defeat: with my weapons, I overthrew the 16,000 soldiers of his army . . . I destroyed numberless towns, devastating them and burning them, and seizing great spoils. . ."

THE ASSYRIAN CIVILIZATION

Language and Literature

The language of the Assyrians, like that of the Babylonians, belonged to the Akkadian group. The only differences between the two languages were some symbols and rules of grammar. Also, both cultures had the same kind of writing; both used the cuneiform script.

Most Assyrians texts that still exist date back to the epoch of the New Empire and were preserved in the famous library of Ashurbanipal in Nineveh. Here this warrior sovereign collected Assyrian, Babylonian, and Sumeric works. Many of these were copies from originals or copies of ancient tablets. These works included legends,

ety was organized in military patterns, in the same way as the army.

Assyrians believed that the king's universal power was the will of the god Assur. Thus, a religious argument was used to justify wars and the cruel deeds that came with them. Gods, feasts, rituals, and myths were the same as those of the Babylonians, and the similarities between the two religions were very great. The city of Assur was dedicated to the god, and the army's feats were also attributed to him. The sovereign was the god's visible representative and also served as the high priest in the religious rituals. Among the main worshipped gods were Ishtar

The bas-reliefs that decorated palace walls depicted scenes of royal life and were mainly related to hunting, wars, or cultural events. They are among the best expressions of Assyrian art. The most famous bas-reliefs are those of the palace of Ashurbanipal in Nineveh. Also notable are the bronze plaques that formed the doors of the palace of Shalmaneser III (858-824 B.C.) and those of the temple of Imgur Enlil which depict the deeds of the king. Also, the official seals showed artistic quality. These seals depicted traditional scenes such as battles, winged spirits, and sacred trees. Despite Babylonian influence, Assyrian art had some unique

The king Tukulti-Ninurta I worships a deity represented by a flame on an altar.

In this bas-relief found in Nimrud, the tree of life stands between two winged spirits with eagles' heads. This scene is tied to the spring feasts that celebrate new growth.

historical accounts, prayers, official deeds, contracts, and commemorative inscriptions. Especially important today are the *Annals,* which are records of the deeds of many sovereigns given in a chronological order. From these writings it is possible to reconstruct Assyrian history from approximately 1000 B.C. These records even offer information on Assyrian war tactics and the loot seized in various battles.

Social and Religious Life

Assyrian law was the most merciless of all the Middle East. The guilty were often punished with beatings or mutilations, and the laws themselves were unrefined and confusing. Soci-

(the god of love and war) and Adad (the god of natural events).

Art

Assyrian art developed unique features during the Middle Empire and reached its height in the period of the New Empire. Architectural works included the ziggurat and the royal palaces. The most beautiful palace was that of King Sargon II in Dur Sharrukin. Sculptures shaped like lions and winged bulls with human heads were a typical feature of the royal palaces. The statues of the kings were highly stylized and did not have any kind of royal posture. Thus, it is difficult to separate them from other figures.

features, especially in its celebration of the empire and the vivid scenes taken from real life. These features are evident in paintings called frescoes that have reached modern times.

Assyrian art is outstanding for its strength and for the kind of world it depicts. The Assyrians were extraordinary stone sculptors and metal artisans, but they were also skilled in working ivory. This was learned when hundreds of ivory objects were discovered during the excavations of Nimrud. These pieces are of great interest, both for their fine crafting and for the themes depicted.

In a specially prepared clearing, a sovereign and his officers battle lions. From evidence furnished by bas-reliefs, it is clear that hunting was among the favorite activities of the Assyrians.

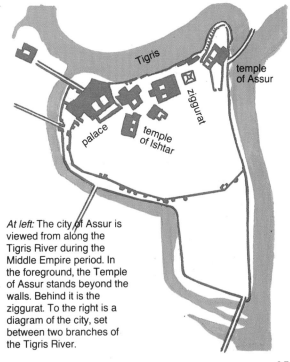

At left: The city of Assur is viewed from along the Tigris River during the Middle Empire period. In the foreground, the Temple of Assur stands beyond the walls. Behind it is the ziggurat. To the right is a diagram of the city, set between two branches of the Tigris River.

THE HURRITES OF URARTU

The name *Urartu,* referring to today's region of Armenia, is first found in Assyrian inscriptions of the thirteenth century B.C. This evidence exists in an account of King Shalmaneser I's recovery of control over seven rebel states in the Urartu region. The Assyrians were very skilled soldiers. But even so, they had problems controlling provinces that were as hard to reach as mountainous Urartu.

In the ninth century, this region was inhabited by Hurrite tribes united under King Aramu. Aramu was defeated by Shalmaneser III. Some scholars believe that the name *Armenia* given later to this area was derived from King Aramu's name.

The Urartean Kings

King Sarduri I moved the capital to Van. King Menua I (810-785 B.C.) expanded his dominion to the west to gain an outlet onto the Mediterranean coast. He built temples, palaces, and towns and encouraged the construction of irrigation systems all over the region. King Argishti I (785-760 B.C.) extended the boundaries of his kingdom even farther and founded the towns of Erebum and of Argishtihinili.

Life in the kingdom of Urartu was affected by the Assyrian presence, which prevented expansion to the west. The Assyrians also constantly invaded the southern part of the kingdom near lakes Urmia and Van. Urartean attempts to expand to the east were stopped by the Medes—Indo-European populations settled there.

In 743 and 735 B.C., Urartu was defeated by Tiglath-pileser II. This marked the beginning of its decline. The kingdom was again sacked in 714 B.C. by Sargon II. Eventually, during the reign of King Sarduri III (645-625 B.C.), the kingdom of Urartu became a state of Assyria. It remained in Assyria's possession until the fall of Nineveh (612 B.C.) caused by the Medes and Scythians. King Rusa III (605-590 B.C.) was the last to leave inscriptions about the major events of his reign. With his death, the kingdom of Urartu collapsed.

Commerce and Agriculture

Hurrite expansion had both military and economic reasons behind it. These people primarily traded iron, silver, and gold objects made with metals coming from the mines of the Taurus region in Cilicia. They also controlled the goods coming from Phoenicia and Syria Minor and from international east-west trade routes. The Hurrites were also skilled metal artisans, and they traded their items over long distances. They increased the productivity of their region through the construction of major irrigation systems. Thus they were able to farm lands which were previously uncultivated.

Architecture and Art

Most of the known architectural works are citadels or fortified towns with large brick walls built on a stone base. Buildings excavated by archaeologists show that a building's ground floor was used as a storage space, while the upper level was used as a home.

Due to the geographical location and features of the kingdom, the art of Urartu was heavily

The Language

The Hurrites spoke an Indo-European language. In their writing, they used cuneiform characters, as did Assyrians and Babylonians. However, the new populations which developed in Armenia after the breakup of the empire abandoned this language and writing. They memorized the events of their history and resorted to the Persian, Aramaic, and Greek languages. This continued until the fifth century A.D. when Saint Mesrop Mashtolz invented the Armenian alphabet. The Armenian language attained great importance among the Indo-European languages. The most ancient Armenian literature is almost entirely formed by translations of Greek works.

influenced by the Assyrians, and partially by the Medes. Bronze objects are almost the only evidence of this art. Large cauldrons were among the most typical objects.

From Urartu to Armenia

After the fall of the Hurrite kingdom, the region was invaded by various tribes coming from the north, such as the Scythians and the Cimmerians. These peoples used the tight network of trade routes when invading the region. A Babylonian inscription from Darius in 520 B.C. still calls the region Urartu; a parallel Persian inscription calls the same region Armenia. In 500 B.C., the Greek geographer Hecataeus spoke of the Armenian population. The terms *Armenia* and *Armenians* were probably originally used by some Iranian tribes, and only later by Romans and Greeks.

This bronze sphinx was part of a throne found in Toprakkale (800-700 B.C.).

MEDITERRANEAN SEA

This drawing shows a storage room with jars for wine and other products on the ground floor of a Urartean house in Karmir Blur.

A cauldron handle shaped like a bull's head comes from Toprakkale.

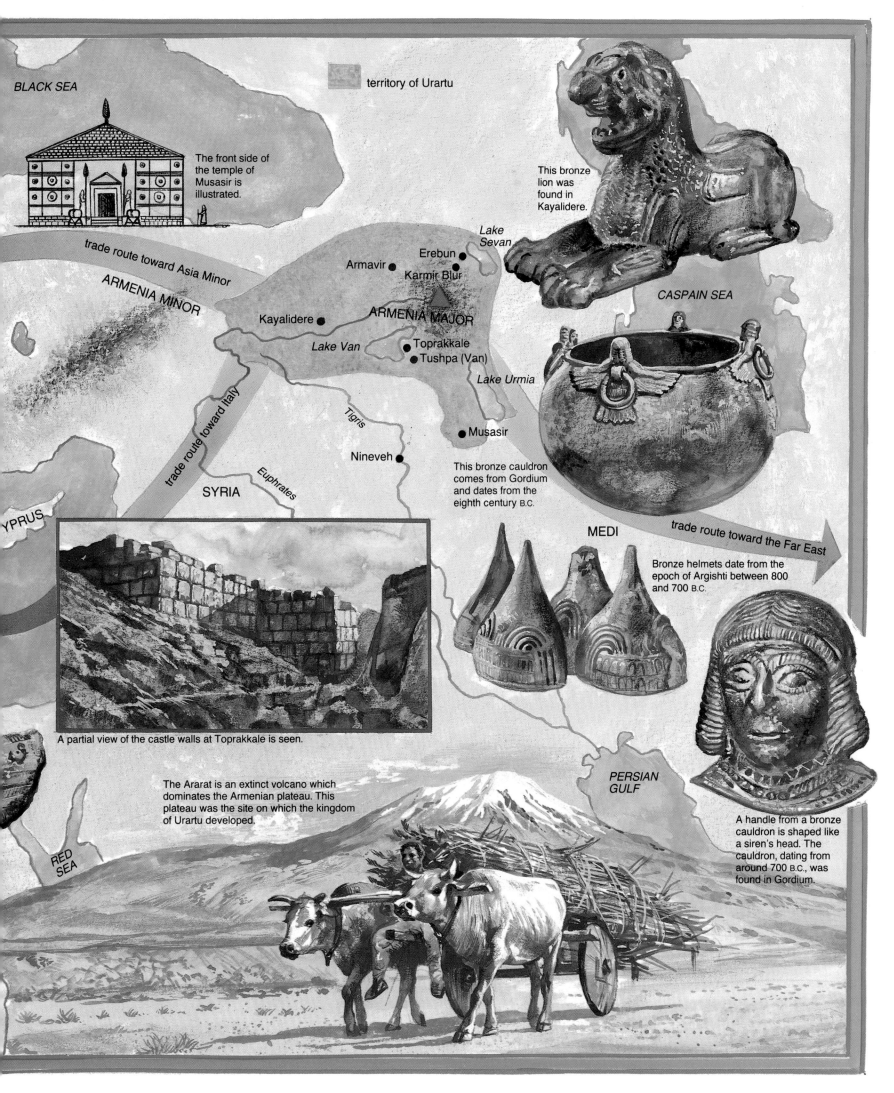

BLACK SEA

The front side of the temple of Musasir is illustrated.

trade route toward Asia Minor

ARMENIA MINOR

trade route toward Italy

Lake Sevan

Erebun

Armavir

Karmir Blur

Kayalidere

ARMENIA MAJOR

Lake Van

Toprakkale

Tushpa (Van)

Lake Urmia

Tigris

Musasir

Nineveh

Euphrates

SYRIA

YPRUS

territory of Urartu

This bronze lion was found in Kayalidere.

CASPAIN SEA

This bronze cauldron comes from Gordium and dates from the eighth century B.C.

MEDI

trade route toward the Far East

Bronze helmets date from the epoch of Argishti between 800 and 700 B.C.

A partial view of the castle walls at Toprakkale is seen.

The Ararat is an extinct volcano which dominates the Armenian plateau. This plateau was the site on which the kingdom of Urartu developed.

RED SEA

PERSIAN GULF

A handle from a bronze cauldron is shaped like a siren's head. The cauldron, dating from around 700 B.C., was found in Gordium.

ANATOLIA IN THE FIRST MILLENNIUM B.C.

By about 1000 B.C., the Anatolia peninsula was populated by massive migrations of people who settled, in successive waves, over a period of several centuries. These populations were of Indo-European origin. Around 1200 B.C., they invaded the territory from the European continent as well as from the sea (the Sea People). Still other populations came from the Eurasian steppes in the following centuries.

With each invasion, towns were destroyed and the countryside was devastated. Often some states would fall while others would take advantage of the situation. For example, the Phrygians contributed to the collapse of the Hittite Empire. Cimmerians after them had the same effect on other states.

The Rise of the Kingdom of the Phrygians

The Phrygia region included the western part of the Anatolian plateau. Around 1200 B.C., this region was invaded by peoples who probably came from Tracia and Macedonia. In the beginning, this area was divided into small kingdoms. These later joined together and formed a powerful, centrally governed kingdom whose capital was Gordium. This state peaked under the rule of King Midas, who fought against the Assyrian king Sargon II and established relationships with Greece. Between 900 and 600 B.C., the Aegean Sea was controlled by the Phrygians. They maintained their independence until they were conquered by the Cimmerians in 695 B.C. The latter, in turn, fell under the power of the Lydians in 585 B.C. Finally, in 546 B.C., the Persian army conquered the whole territory.

The Culture of the Phrygians

Phrygian art has come to light in excavations in the towns of Gordium, Eskisehir, Ancira, Alaca, Kültepe, and Bogazköy. Among the typical monuments are tombs and temples decorated with lions and geometrical patterns. Burial mounds containing precious objects were found in Gordium. The use of bronze and ivory was a typical feature of Phrygian art.

The Phrygians spoke an Indo-European language that is known through stone carvings and inscriptions. The oldest inscriptions were found near Gordium and date back to 600 B.C. A more recent form of Phrygian language, called Neo-Phrygian, developed around 300 B.C. and was used in inscriptions found south of Gordium. The Phrygian alphabet was very similar to that of ancient Greek.

The Kingdom of Lydia

Lydia included the western and southern part of Anatolia. It had an ancient history and was highly civilized. It was also an important trade center because of the many gulfs on its coast facing the Aegean Sea. The Lydians were probably a people of Indo-European origin, but the date of their arrival in the region is uncertain. They were first mentioned in accounts from the seventh century B.C.

The Heraclidae dynasty ruled Lydia for 505 years. The last king of the Heraclidae dynasty was Candaules, who was killed in 685 B.C. by Gyges. Gyges then founded the Mermnads dynasty. The last king of this dynasty was Croesus (560-546 B.C.), under whose guidance Lydia became a true empire. It stretched over territories on both sides of the Halys River and included the Greek towns of the Ionia region. Croesus reigned until 546 B.C. when King Cyrus of Persia conquered Lydia.

The Lydians were wealthy and sophisticated. They already used currency in the seventh century B.C. The art of the Lydians followed Greek and eastern models, with favorite figures being lions and sphinxes. Particularly interesting are the hundreds of huge burial mounds.

The Lycians

The southeastern extremity of Asia Minor is covered by a plateau and by mountain chains. Before the Greeks arrived, this area was inhabited by the Lycians. According to the Greek historian Herodotus, the Lycians were a pirate people native to the island of Crete. In the sixth century B.C., the region became part of the Persian Empire.

The Lycian language was an Indo-European language that has not yet been completely decoded. Examples of it are provided by inscriptions dating from between 500 and 300 B.C. The only examples of Lycian art are grave monuments that were found in the region's main towns.

On the large map, the kingdoms of Anatolia are presented. The small map traces migrations of Indo-European populations.

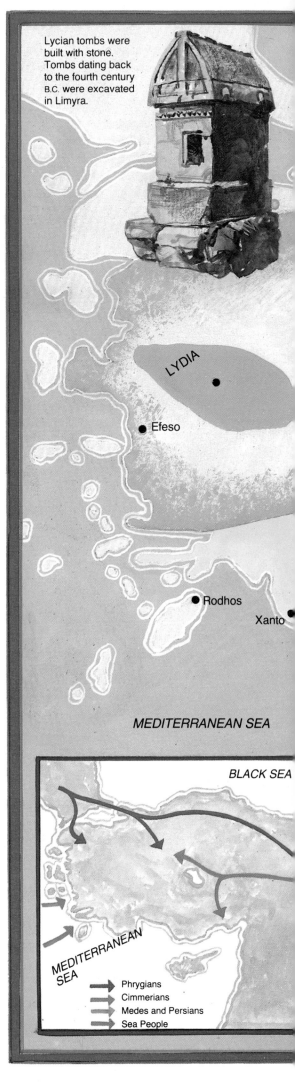

Lycian tombs were built with stone. Tombs dating back to the fourth century B.C. were excavated in Limyra.

LYDIA

Efeso

Rodhos

Xanto

MEDITERRANEAN SEA

BLACK SEA

MEDITERRANEAN SEA

→ Phrygians
→ Cimmerians
→ Medes and Persians
→ Sea People

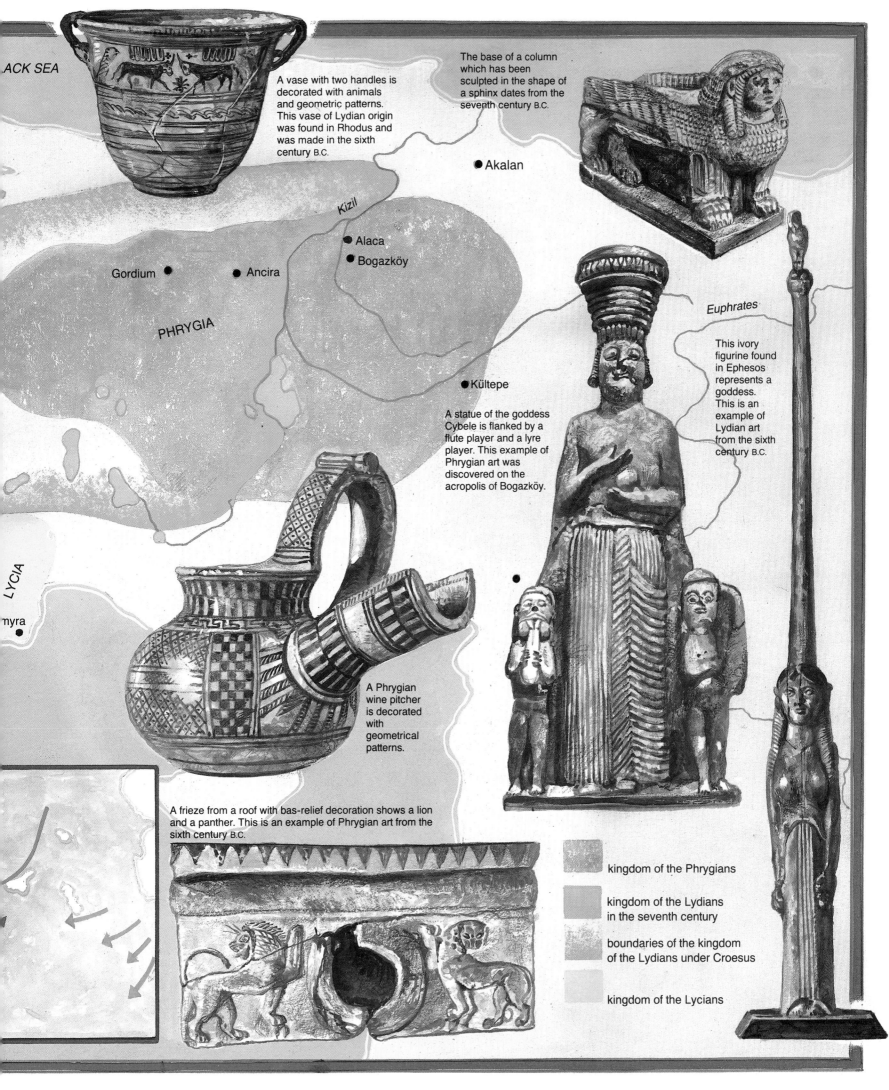

BLACK SEA

A vase with two handles is decorated with animals and geometric patterns. This vase of Lydian origin was found in Rhodus and was made in the sixth century B.C.

The base of a column which has been sculpted in the shape of a sphinx dates from the seventh century B.C.

● Akalan

Kizil

● Alaca
● Bogazköy

Gordium ●   ● Ancira

PHRYGIA

Euphrates

● Kültepe

This ivory figurine found in Ephesos represents a goddess. This is an example of Lydian art from the sixth century B.C.

A statue of the goddess Cybele is flanked by a flute player and a lyre player. This example of Phrygian art was discovered on the acropolis of Bogazköy.

LYCIA

myra

A Phrygian wine pitcher is decorated with geometrical patterns.

A frieze from a roof with bas-relief decoration shows a lion and a panther. This is an example of Phrygian art from the sixth century B.C.

kingdom of the Phrygians

kingdom of the Lydians in the seventh century

boundaries of the kingdom of the Lydians under Croesus

kingdom of the Lycians

39

The Hebrews enter the town of Jerusalem after conquering it.

The temple erected by King Solomon was reconstructed according to the description which is given of it in the Book of the Kings.

ISRAEL—
THE PERIOD OF THE KINGS TO EXILE

When the Hebrews occupied Canaan, they preferred to settle in sparsely populated hilly areas. They avoided the urban settlements, which were then in the hands of the Canaanites, as well as the fortified towns, often ruled by Philistine tribes. The region's coastal areas were divided among Canaanites and Philistines.

Religion was the great element of unity among the Twelve Tribes of Israelites. This religion, however, also presented an element of weakness for the people. Due to its peculiarities, such as the worshipping of a single god and the absence of representations of that god, the religion was constantly in danger of being absorbed within the local polytheistic religion.

The Kings

The figure of the Hebrew king was greatly different from that of any other king in the ancient world. His legislative power was very limited. For one thing, he was the enforcer of divine laws more than a lawmaker. The first king, appointed by Samuel, was Saul, a member of the tribe of Benjamin. Backed by his people, Saul undertook a series of victorious battles against the Philistines and other enemies who lived in the Hebrew territory. Unfortunately, Saul died on the battlefield with his son, Jonathan.

David, of the tribe of Judah, succeeded Saul and ruled from 1010-970 B.C. David was the greatest king of Israel. He brilliantly ended the war against the Philistines, expanded the kingdom's boundaries both to the north and to the south, and gave the twelve tribes a kingdom so vast that it remained unequaled in Hebrew history. David, also a shrewd politician, sought to unify the tribes. For his capital, he chose a town which was not yet inhabited by any tribe and occupied it himself. The town, called Jebus, was later called Jerusalem. In Jerusalem, David chose the sites where the Temple, the royal palace, and all the administration buildings were to be erected. The construction was completed by David's son and successor, Solomon, who ruled from 970-931 B.C. Solomon divided the kingdom into provinces, or military districts, strengthened the border towns with fortresses, and greatly improved sea trade.

The Division of the Kingdom: Israel and Judah

Upon Solomon's death, the tribes of the northern areas broke away from the dynasty of David and from Jerusalem. Thus the country was divided into two kingdoms: the kingdom of Israel to the north, and that of Judah to the south. The first king of the northern kingdom was Jeroboam (931-910 B.C.). The southern kingdom was ruled by Solomon's son Rehoboam (931-913 B.C.).

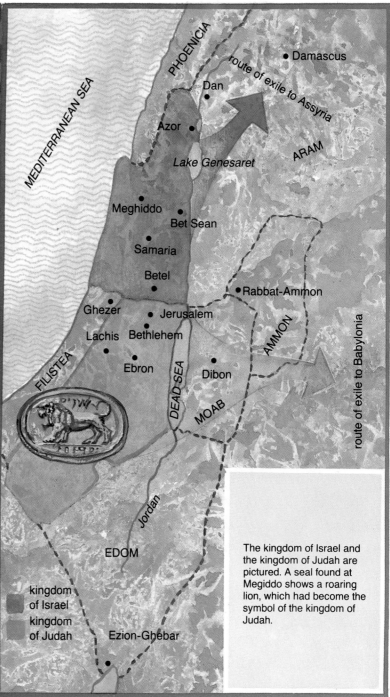

The kingdom of Israel and the kingdom of Judah are pictured. A seal found at Megiddo shows a roaring lion, which had become the symbol of the kingdom of Judah.

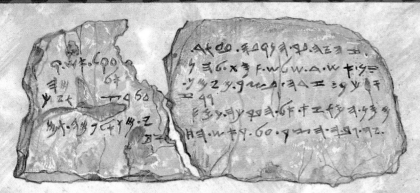

Ancient Evidence of Hebrew Writing

This inscription, carved on a rock, celebrates the excavation of the Siloan tunnel near Jerusalem. It is the oldest known inscription in the Hebrew language. It dates back to 701 B.C. The translation reads as follows: "This is the boring [perforation]. And this is how the perforation was accomplished when only three cubits [about 60 inches/150 cm] remained to be perforated, pick ax against pick ax, one against the other. When only three cubits remained to be perforated, the men calling each other could hear each other's voices because there was a crack in the rock, from right to left. In this way, on the day of the perforation, the miners struck one against the other, pick ax against pick ax. And the waters began to flow from the spring into the pool, for a distance of 1,200 cubits [1,752 feet/534 m]. The layer of rock above the heads of the miners was 100 cubits thick [820 feet/250 m]."

The northern kingdom was much more wealthy and powerful than the southern kingdom, but it was troubled by internal problems. One problem was the struggle for royal power, with several families trying to get control. Different families were continually succeeding each other in the northern kingdom. Another problem troubling the kingdom was a series of fierce religious fights between the followers of the traditional religion and those who wanted to grant increasing space to Canaanite deities and rituals. The most important kings of the north were: Ahab (874-853 B.C.), who married the Canaanite woman Jezebel and opposed the pro-phet Elijah; Joram (852-841 B.C.) and Jehu (841-814 B.C.), who led a war against King Mesha of Moab; Menahem (743-738 B.C.) and Pekah (737-732 B.C.), who headed the clashes with the Assyrian king Tiglath-pileser III and were defeated; and finally, Hoshea (732-724 B.C.). Under Hoshea's rule, Samaria, the capital, was attacked by King Shalmaneser V. Eventually, the northern kingdom was defeated and its people were deported by Sargon II in 721 B.C.

The End of Judah

The life of the kingdom of Judah was more peaceful. Its most important kings were: Hezekiah (716-687 B.C.), who lost some towns to Sargon II and endured the siege of Jerusalem; Manasseh (687-642 B.C.), who had to pay tribute to the Assyrian kings Esarhaddon and Ashurbanipal; and Josiah (640-609 B.C.), who began a vast religious reform and died in battle against the Egyptian pharaoh Neco II. In this period, the Babylonian Empire regained its strength, and the Assyrian epoch was coming to an end. The New Babylonian king Nebuchadnezzar finally crushed the kingdom of Judah and deported the Hebrew population to Babylonia.

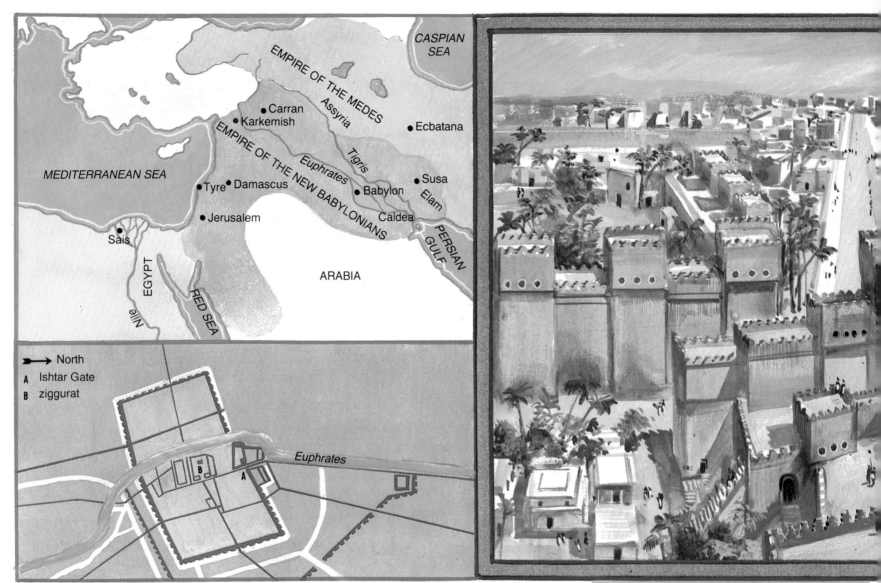

At the top is a map of the New Babylonian Empire. At the bottom is a plan of the city of Babylon along the Euphrates River between 700 and 500 B.C.

→ North
A Ishtar Gate
B ziggurat

THE BRIEF DOMINION OF THE BABYLONIANS

In spite of constant Assyrian victories and expansion, the Assyrian Empire's northern, southern, and eastern frontiers were constantly exposed to attacks from new populations. The ceaseless wars brought wealth to the empire but exhausted the population. The king Ashurbanipal repressed many attacks on the empire, including those on the region of Elam which formed its southern part. After the king's death in 631 B.C., however, the empire collapsed and never regained its strength. In 626 B.C., the Chaldaean general Nabopolassar seized Babylon and proclaimed its independence from the Assyrian Empire. He founded the XI Chaldaean dynasty, also called the New Babylonian dynasty. In 616 B.C., he declared war on Assyria and made an alliance with the Medes. The Egyptian pharaoh Psammetichus joined the war on the side of Assyria, but the city of Nineveh fell before his arrival in 612 B.C.

The Assyrian and Egyptian armies clashed against the armies of the Medes and of Nabopolassar at Carchemish in 605 B.C. This was the last great battle fought by the Assyrians. In it, the young general of Nabopolassar, Nebuchadnezzar, proved his great courage. After the battle, the Egyptians went back to their homeland, while New Babylonians and Medes, led by King Cyaxares, renewed their alliance and agreed to completely destroy the Assyrian kingdom.

Nebuchadnezzar's Kingdom

Under Nabopolassar's successor, Nebuchadnezzar (605-562 B.C.), the New Babylonian kingdom reached its greatest splendor. The king enlarged the territory that he had inherited, conquering Syria, the city of Tyre, and all of Phoenicia. He also conquered the kingdom of Judah, in Palestine, destroying Jerusalem and its Temple in 587 B.C. From the Assyrians, Nebuchadnezzar learned the practice of moving the defeated nobles, aristocrats, and traders from their homeland.

Nabonidus: The Last Gleam

The reign of Nebuchadnezzar was followed

Builder Kings

The first New Babylonian kings were very active builders. They put all of their energy into the reconstruction of the capital, Babylon. They erected a double wall around the city, which was located on the Euphrates River. Inside the defensive walls were splendid living quarters and terraces. Babylon is famous for the beautiful hanging gardens created on some of the terraces. The ziggurat, a monument later called the Tower of Babel, and its temple to the god Marduk, dominated the entire city.

Nebuchadnezzar's works were celebrated in an inscription as follows: "I have completed the construction of Babylon, the sublime city / the city of his majesty (Marduk) / and its great walls. / By its entrance doors I have put giant bulls, / a thing that no one had ever done before. / My father surrounded the city with two walls made of tar and fired bricks, / I erected a third strong wall, made of tar and fired bricks / and joined it to the walls of my father.

A view of Babylon shows the Ishtar Gate and an avenue called the Processional Street. In the upper right corner, the hanging gardens and the ziggurat with the Temple of Marduk can be seen.

Panels of colored brick depict two symbolic animals: the lion of the Processional Street and the dragon of the Ishtar Gate (panels of enameled tiles).

Shown here is an illustration of the ziggurat of Babylon. This building was called "the house of the foundations of heaven and earth." It was over 295 feet (90 m) high and was topped with a small temple. This temple was the permanent residence of Marduk, the god of the city.

by a brief period of decline that ended in the empire's final collapse. The last New Babylonian king was Nabonidus (556-539 B.C.). He vainly resisted the increasing power of the Persians and retreated for a certain time to the oasis of Teiman on the Arabian border. This retreat was the origin of several legends. One legend holds that the king made this retreat because of a mystical crisis. Today, it seems more likely that he tried to organize Arabic tribes to defend the New Babylonian Empire. On the other hand, Nabonidus had made religious reforms, resulting in disagreement with the priests. The priests thus cherished the eventual defeat of this heretic king when the Persian king Cyrus invaded New Babylonia in 539 B.C. Entering the city of Babylon without striking a blow, Cyrus ended the short period of the New Babylonian kingdom.

Culture and Society

The culture and art of the Babylonians always held a position of great prestige in ancient Mesopotamia. The Babylonians maintained this position during most of the epoch of the Persian Empire, and their influence was evident in writing, language, philosophy, and religion. Their literature was extremely rich, and many of their documents still exist. The Babylonian society was organized in a pyramidal structure. At the top was the king, who was the supreme military, religious, and political leader. The economy of the kingdom was based on agriculture, livestock-raising, and artisan activities that were sometimes highly specialized. Commercial trading, both by river and by land, was greatly developed.

THE PERSIANS

The Arrival of Iranian Populations

The name *Persians* is mentioned for the first time in Assyrian documents of the ninth century B.C. At that time, nomadic tribes of Medes and Persians had settled on the Iranian plateau (territory that includes parts of modern Iran and Afghanistan) where they lived as shepherds and farmers. By the seventh century B.C., the Medes had established the kingdom of Media on the northern end of the plateau and conquered the Persians who had settled to the south. From there, the Medes moved west and conquered Susa and the lands of Elam. Toward the end of the seventh century B.C., the Medes fought against the Assyrians, in alliance with the Babylonians. Nineveh, Assyria's capital, fell in 612 B.C. Soon afterward all of Assyria was conquered.

About 550 B.C., the Persians, led by Cyrus the Great, overthrew the Medes. With the Median lands in their possession, the Persians established a very powerful empire. Cyrus, who was a member of the Achaemenid dynasty, became its first ruler. (Thus the empire was called the Achaemenid Empire.) Ecbatana, the capital of Media, became the summer residence of the court of the Achaemenid. The ancient city of Pasargadae became the sacred city of the Achaemenid, and Cyrus ordered that his tomb be erected there.

Under Cyrus the Great, Anatolia also became a Persian province. Later, the regions of Sogdiana and Bactria were added to the empire. In 539 B.C., the New Babylonian kingdom was defeated, and still later the populations of Syria, Phoenicia, and Palestine were subjugated.

The Empire Expands

Cyrus's son, Cambyses II, became his successor. Cambyses expanded the empire's territory to include Egypt and Cyrenaica, but he also had to cope with numerous rebellions. Darius I, who became king in 522 B.C., eventually con-

quered the rebellious provinces and put an end to the turmoil. First, he enlarged the kingdom's eastern borders as far as the upper reaches of the Indus River. Then he turned west and conquered Tracia and Macedonia. He also conducted an unsuccessful campaign against the Scythians in the region of the lower reaches of the Danube. Meanwhile, the Persians had their eyes on Greece and the treasures contained in the Greek sanctuaries. Darius declared war against Athens, but the hostilities were concluded in Marathon with the victory of the Athenians in 490 B.C. Darius died in 486 B.C.

In 486 B.C., Xerxes I succeeded his father Darius. He soon reestablished Persian power and prestige in the western provinces. He regained control of Thrace and Macedonia and also penetrated into Boeotia and Thessaly. Leonidas, king of Sparta, tried to stop Xerxes at Thermopylae, north of Athens, but was defeated. Athens was conquered in 480 B.C. However, shortly after, in the Battle of Salamis, the Greek fleet ambushed the Persian navy, destroying about half of the fleet. At this point, Xerxes' drive to control Greece had lost strength. He returned home to Persia, leaving his general, Mardonius, in command. A final battle took place at Plataea in 479 B.C. There the Greeks again defeated the Persian army and put an end to the invasion.

Xerxes' death in 465 B.C. signaled a decline for the Achaemenid Empire. Although the empire continued to exist, it was plagued by constant struggles, military clashes, and internal problems. Finally, in 331 B.C., Alexander the Great led the Macedonians to a victory over the Persian army in the Battle of Arbela. With this defeat, the Achaemenid Empire came to an end.

At right: The map depicts the Achaemenid Empire at its peak under Darius (522-486 B.C.). *Top and bottom of page:* Shown is part of the frieze which decorated the staircase of the famous palace of Persepolis, the capital of the empire founded by Darius I around 516 B.C. and enlarged by his son Xerxes. The frieze depicts a procession of delegates from the twenty-eight conquered nations bringing gifts to the king. *On top:* Elamites bring a lion, while the Babylonians offer a buffalo. *Below:* The Lydians are seen at the left. To the right, the eastern Iranians offer a camel.

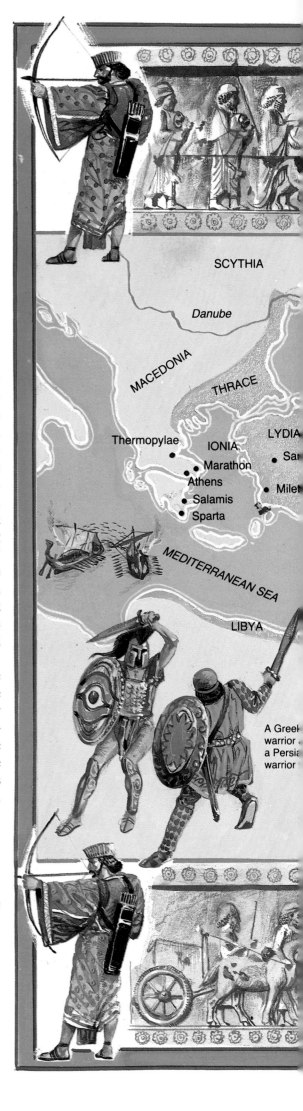

SCYTHIA

Danube

MACEDONIA

THRACE

LYDIA

Thermopylae

IONIA

Sar

Marathon

Athens

Mile

Salamis

Sparta

MEDITERRANEAN SEA

LIBYA

A Greek warrior a Persia warrior

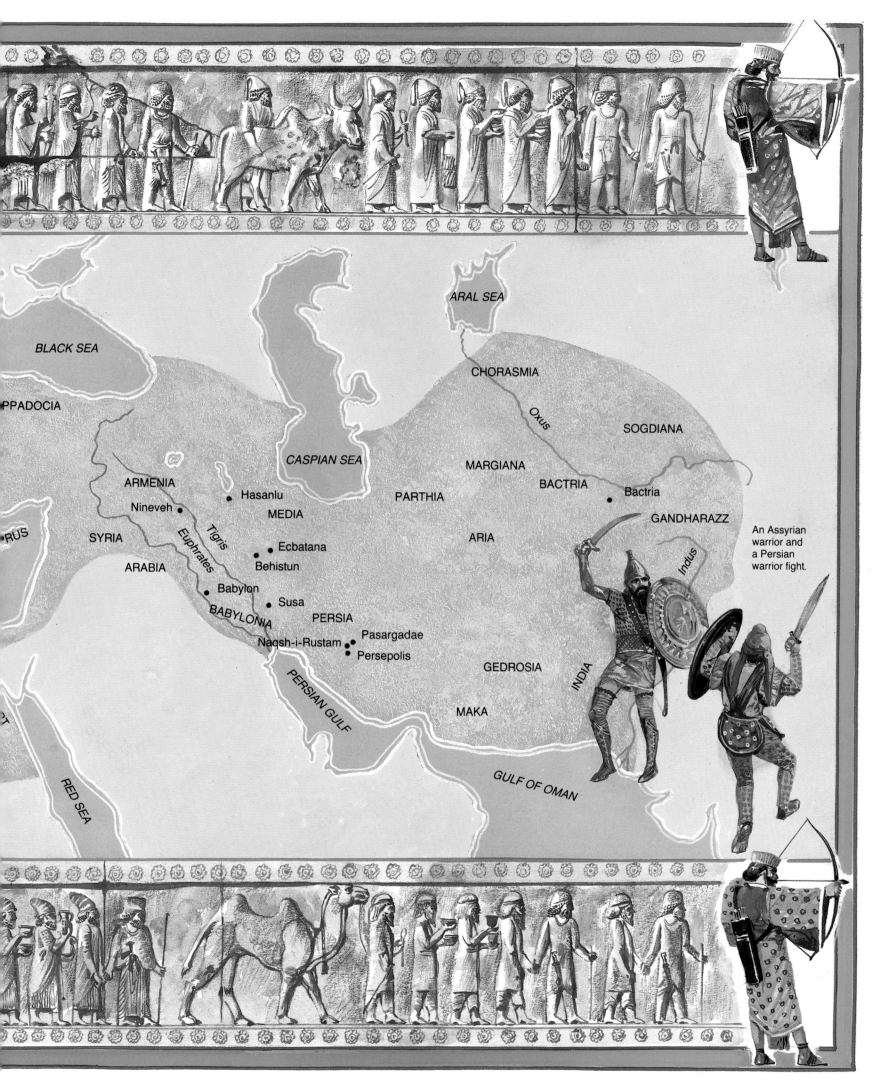

BLACK SEA

PPADOCIA

ARAL SEA

CHORASMIA

Oxus

SOGDIANA

CASPIAN SEA

MARGIANA

ARMENIA

Hasanlu

PARTHIA

BACTRIA

Bactria

Nineveh

MEDIA

GANDHARAZZ

RUS

SYRIA

Tigris

Euphrates

Ecbatana

ARIA

Indus

An Assyrian
warrior and
a Persian
warrior fight.

ARABIA

Behistun

Babylon

Susa

BABYLONIA

PERSIA

Pasargadae

Naqsh-i-Rustam

Persepolis

GEDROSIA

INDIA

MAKA

PERSIAN GULF

RED SEA

GULF OF OMAN

THE POLITICAL POWER OF THE ACHAEMENID EMPIRE

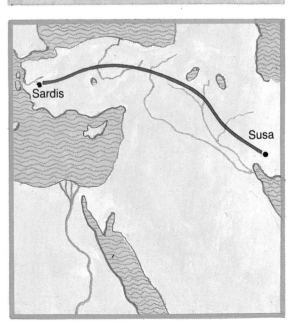

The Achaemenid Empire began with Cyrus the Great and was characterized by great mercy. This quality was a novelty in a region where memories of fierce Assyrian rule were still alive. Conquered princes were not tortured or killed. In fact, they were sometimes given positions within the empire's administration. The king's authority was absolute, but he was helped by an assembly of nobles. People of the most varied nationalities were part of the imperial administration. Only the army was composed mainly of Medes and Persians.

Taxes were collected fairly, although Medes and Persians were granted a certain degree of privilege in their payments. The various con-

increasing their trade. Moreover, improved roads allowed for rapid communication throughout the empire. An example of this is the famous Royal Road which connected Susa, in the heart of the empire, to Sardis, in Lydia, covering a distance of over 1,491 miles (2,400 km). This road was safe, furnished with sites where horses could be replaced, and travelers could eat and rest.

The First Great Empire

Under kings Cyrus the Great and Darius I, the Persians conquered many of the ancient civilizations, absorbing them into their empire. For the first time in history, Mesopotamia,

The King of Kings

Darius I ordered that two tablets, a gold one and a silver one, be placed within the foundations of the palace of Persepolis in remembrance of its construction. The text, written in ancient Persian, in Babylonian, and in Elamite, reads as follows: "This is the kingdom which I own, stretching from the country of the Saka people, who live on this side of the Sogdiana, to the country of Kush, from India to Sardis. Here is what Ahura Mazda has bestowed on me, he who is the foremost of all the gods. May Ahura Mazda protect me and my family."

At left, above: A rock bas-relief from the sixth century B.C. shows the likeness of Darius I. It was found in Behistun.

The illustration above is of a horse changing station along the Ro Road. *Map to the left:* The Royal Road connected Sardis, located near the Mediterranean Sea, to Susa, one of the four capitals of t Achaemenid Empire.

quered populations were allowed to retain their religions, laws, customs, and sometimes even their leaders, provided they recognized the authority of the king. The empire was divided into provinces, called satrapies. Each satrapy was ruled by a "protector of the kingdom." This protector administered justice, maintained order, and collected taxes. He was also the commander of the local troops, with the exception of the larger ones. Larger forces were led by a general who was responsible to the king.

Within the empire, major efforts were made to accomplish public works. These included drainage of swampy areas, the installation of irrigation systems, and road construction. The Persians were the first to use camels as transport animals. As a result, they established relationships with peoples of remote areas, notably

The Persian Language

The Persian language is an Indo-European language, very close to the Sanskrit language. In its ancient form, it was written with cuneiform characters, as shown by the rock inscriptions of the period between kings Darius and Artaxerxes III (from 600-300 B.C.). It was based on an Iranian dialect used by the court.

Another form of Persian language is the Avestan. This was the refined language used in sacred texts (called *Avesta*) which contained the doctrine of Zoroaster. The language, which was used between 250 B.C. and A.D. 650, is called Middle Persian or Pahlavi. This is a complex language which was used to write the commentaries upon the *Avesta*. The common language spoken throughout the empire from Egypt to India was Aramaic, a language of the Semitic group.

Darius I meets with representatives of foreign populations.

Syria, Egypt, Asia Minor, numerous Greek towns, and part of India were united under one king. The Persians did not impose their civilization on the populations of their empire. Such an action would have caused the regression of very ancient civilizations, which were more advanced than the Persian civilization. Cyrus and Darius granted wide freedom to the different territories and favored the preservation of the different cultures. This political policy resulted in sharp cultural differences between the Persians and the conquered peoples. These differences eventually led to the empire's fall.

But this policy had great historical importance. The principles by which the Persions ruled this empire of many cultures were to remain alive even after the empire had fallen. Alexander the Great adopted them, and from the Hellenistic world, they were eventually transmitted to modern Europe.

THE PERSIAN GOVERNMENT

KING OF THE KINGS

COUNCIL OF THE EMPEROR
Formed by nobles representing all peoples of the empire

SATRAPS
Usually veteran generals; one at the head of each large province, or satrapy; heads of the civilians and of local armies

GENERALS
Commanders of the royal troops; formed of Median and Persian soldiers; stationed at the various satrapies

POPULATIONS OF THE EMPIRE
Each population ruled by its own laws, traditions, and customs and led by its own heads

PERSIAN RELIGION AND ART

This building was found near the royal tombs of Naqsh-i-Rustam.

This altar, discovered in Naqsh-i-Rustam, dates back to the third century B.C.

The magi were priests of the ancient Persian religion. This drawing was inspired by a gold plate found near the Oxus River. The plate dates from between 700 and 500 B.C.

Religion

The Persian religion was extremely rich. According to tradition, it was inspired by the doctrine of Zoroaster, a priest who lived around 600 B.C. Zoroaster preached for changes and improvements in the ancient Iranian religion. Gradually, Zoroaster developed a small group of followers. He required that his followers abandon the ancient tradition of sacrificing a bull to the gods. Knowledge of his teachings comes through the sacred texts, called *Avesta*, which have been preserved to present times.

The core of Zoroaster's doctrine and preaching is morality, which is people's behavior and actions. He was obsessed by the idea that the wicked would be punished, and the virtuous would be rewarded. He taught that each person was free to choose, and that in choosing the way of the god Ahura Mazda, one was making the right choice. At the end of life, each human being would be judged according to the choices he or she had made. Those who had made the right choices would be welcomed into paradise. Sinners would dwell in the house of evil forever.

Ahura Mazda was the just and supreme god who constantly fought against evil. He would triumph at the end of times. In addition to this god, who was always depicted emerging from a winged solar disk, the gods Mithra and Anahit were also worshipped. These three gods formed the triad of the Persian religion. As Ahura Mazda's representative, the Persian king's responsibility was to see that justice triumphed at all times. He was also to allow all people to live according to their own laws. These religious concepts might have influenced Cyrus's decision to allow the Jewish people, who were exiled in Babylonia, to return to their homeland.

The Art

Early Iranian art bore reminders of the art of the steppe tribes. Examples were discovered during archaeological excavations in numerous necropolises (cemeteries). The necropolis of Siyalk is made up of tombs of people from all social classes. Excavations in this necropolis revealed bangles, earrings, and ceramics decorated with geometrical patterns, and animal and human figures. The tombs of Khurvin show different artistic tendencies, while excavations in Hasanlu revealed art objects with fantastic shapes.

The most outstanding art forms produced by these early Iranian populations were highly original bronze and iron objects from Luristan during the seventh century B.C. Through these materials, the artists expressed an extraordinarily elaborate mythology. During the two centuries of the Achaemenid dynasty, Persian art showed aulic features. This means that the art was meant to celebrate and praise the monarchy and to enhance the feeling of belonging to a unique political entity. The artists were influenced by art forms of various lands of the empire, especially by Mesopotamian art.

Since the Persians were great builders of towns, courts, and religious sites, knowledge of their art has been known mainly through the ruins of the various capitals: Ecbatana, Pasargadae, Susa, and Persepolis. In each capital, the central and most important monument was the royal palace, which was used as a residence, a treasury, and a site for reception and public audiences. At the center of the palace was the audience chamber, with its ceiling supported by several rows of columns. The palace was decorated with winged bulls, figures of spirits, monumental staircases, and bas-reliefs depicting processions and ceremonies.

Near Persepolis, in Naqsh-i-Rustam, a sanctuary from an earlier period became a burial site under the Achaemenid. Four caves dug in the rocky outcropping were the tombs of Darius, Xerxes, Artaxerxes I, and Darius II.

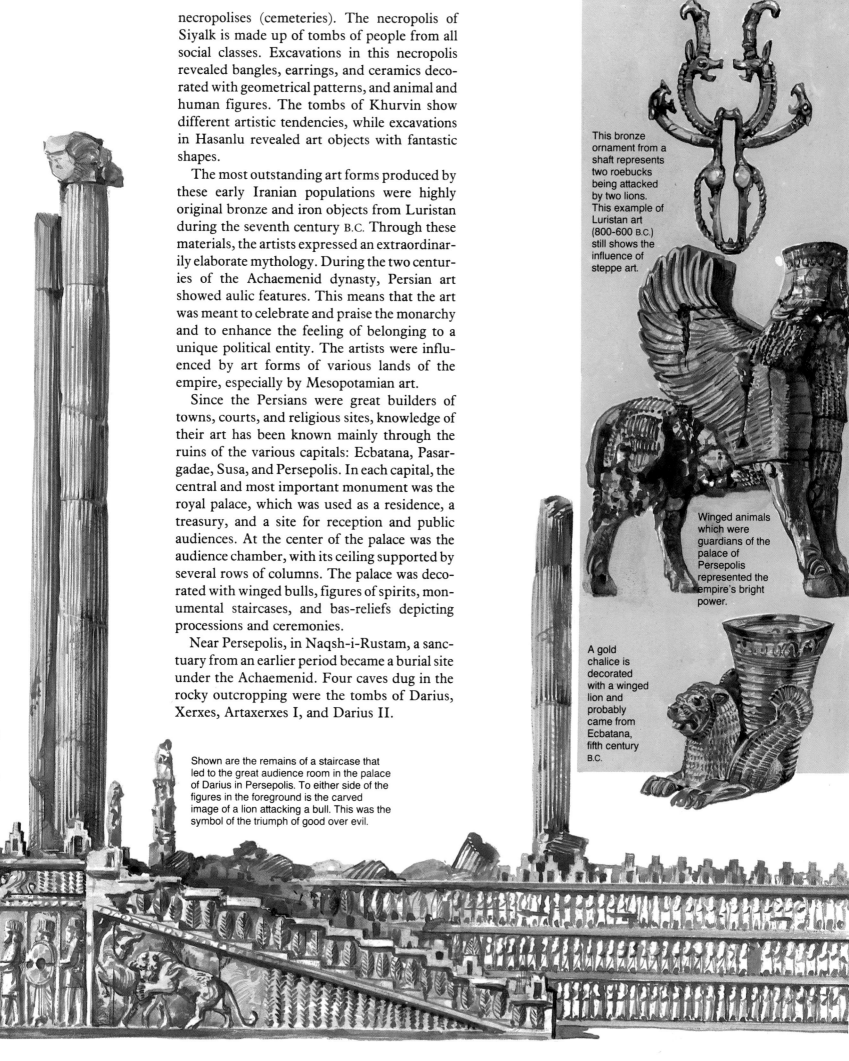

This bronze ornament from a shaft represents two roebucks being attacked by two lions. This example of Luristan art (800-600 B.C.) still shows the influence of steppe art.

Winged animals which were guardians of the palace of Persepolis represented the empire's bright power.

A gold chalice is decorated with a winged lion and probably came from Ecbatana, fifth century B.C.

Shown are the remains of a staircase that led to the great audience room in the palace of Darius in Persepolis. To either side of the figures in the foreground is the carved image of a lion attacking a bull. This was the symbol of the triumph of good over evil.

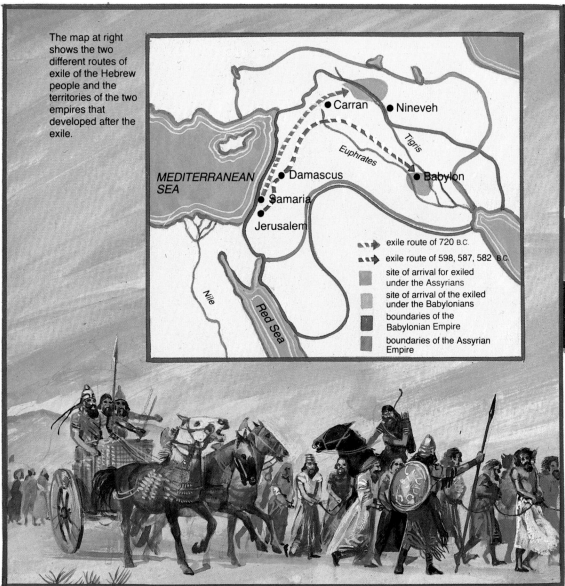

The map at right shows the two different routes of exile of the Hebrew people and the territories of the two empires that developed after the exile.

MEDITERRANEAN SEA

Carran • Nineveh

Euphrates

Tigris

Damascus

Babylon

Samaria

Jerusalem

Nile

Red Sea

- - → exile route of 720 B.C.
- - → exile route of 598, 587, 582 B.C.
☐ site of arrival for exiled under the Assyrians
☐ site of arrival of the exiled under the Babylonians
☐ boundaries of the Babylonian Empire
☐ boundaries of the Assyrian Empire

Above: This scene depicts the deportation of the Hebrews to Babylonia. *Top, middle:* Life in exile soon took on the normal features of daily life. The Hebrews who wanted to remain faithful to their homeland performed the activities of the other people around them but kept the memory of the lost homeland.

A stone is carved with Babylonian deities. It comes from the twelfth century B.C.

THE EXILE AND RETURN OF THE HEBREWS

Israel's Exile in Assyria

When the Assyrian king Sargon II expanded the Assyrian Empire in the eighth century B.C., the conquered territory included the kingdom of Israel. Sargon then uprooted the population of Israel and sent other people to settle in the region, thus eliminating most of the tradition of the northern kingdom. Some of the Hebrews mingled with the people of their new country. Others gathered into Hebrew communities that survived under the different sovereigns who ruled northern Mesopotamia. Still other Hebrews went back to their home country during the period of Persian domination.

The Exile in Babylonia

In the sixth century B.C. the Babylonians captured Judah and took many of its people prisoner. The people, including priests, royal administrators, intellectuals, artisans, and traders, were deported to Babylonia in a period that came to be called the Babylonian Exile.

Once in the country of exile, the Hebrews tried to make the best of their fate, in the hope that they would eventually return to their homeland. This period of exile was a time of great reflection. The people tried to understand the religious consequences of events that had forced them to choose between keeping their culture alive and separate, or mingling with the people of the new country. Unlike the people of the northern kingdom, the people of Judah chose to keep the tradition alive.

The prophet Ezekiel voiced the people's con-

The Hebrew Bible

During the exile in Babylonia and in the following centuries, texts containing the revealed word of the God of Israel, Yahweh, took on their final form. This was achieved in various ways. The most ancient papyrus and leather rolls, which the priests and the scribes had salvaged from destruction, were copied. Parts of the revelation that had been passed on orally were then written down.

The Hebrew Bible is made up of The Law, which consists of the five

Back in Jerusalem, the Hebrews rebuilt the walls and the altar, where sacrifices were again performed.

The siege of Babylon in 539 B.C. is depicted on this clay cylinder.

books of the Pentateuch (Genesis, Exodus, Leviticus, Numbers, and Deuteronomy); the Prophets; and the Hagiograph (which among others includes the Psalms, the book of Job, the Proverbs, and the Song of Songs). The first Christians realized that these books contained an essential part of the revelation of God to humans but added still other texts which the Hebrews did not know. These texts all together formed the Old Testament.

flicting thoughts on this matter. Ezekiel was a priest who had been deported in his youth and had grown up in Babylon with his heart in the motherland. But he dreamed of a completely different homeland than the one he had known. The new Judah was a country without a king, centered around the Temple, strictly abiding by the law of Moses. Under the direction of a High Priest, there would be a strict distinction between Hebrews and non-Hebrews. These principles surfaced during the period following the exile; they became the basis of the new nation of Israel.

The Return and the Reconstruction

In 538 B.C., the Persian king Cyrus conquered Babylonia. He then issued a decree allowing the exiled people to return to their homelands. The events beyond this are very vague, and no certain historical reports exist. In the beginning, the homecomers, who were few in number, faced many difficulties. First, the land was either uncultivated or in the hands of other peoples, and survival was not easy. Moreover, all of the people wanted to erect a new temple from the ruins, but it was first necessary to build an altar for sacrifices.

The first appointed high commissioner was Zerubbabel, a descendant from the family of David, and the High Priest was Joshua. The prophets who inspired the rebirth of Israel were Haggai and Zechariah. The protector of the Hebrew law of Moses was the scribe Ezra. Probably between 445-443 B.C., Nehemiah first visited Jerusalem. He was intensely involved in reconstructing Jerusalem. He was equally interested in social reform on the basis of the laws that had been written during the exile and in the hope of a rebirth of the nation of Israel. The reconstruction was tied to the two great personalities of Ezra and Nehemiah, who together with Ezekiel are considered the founders of Judaism.

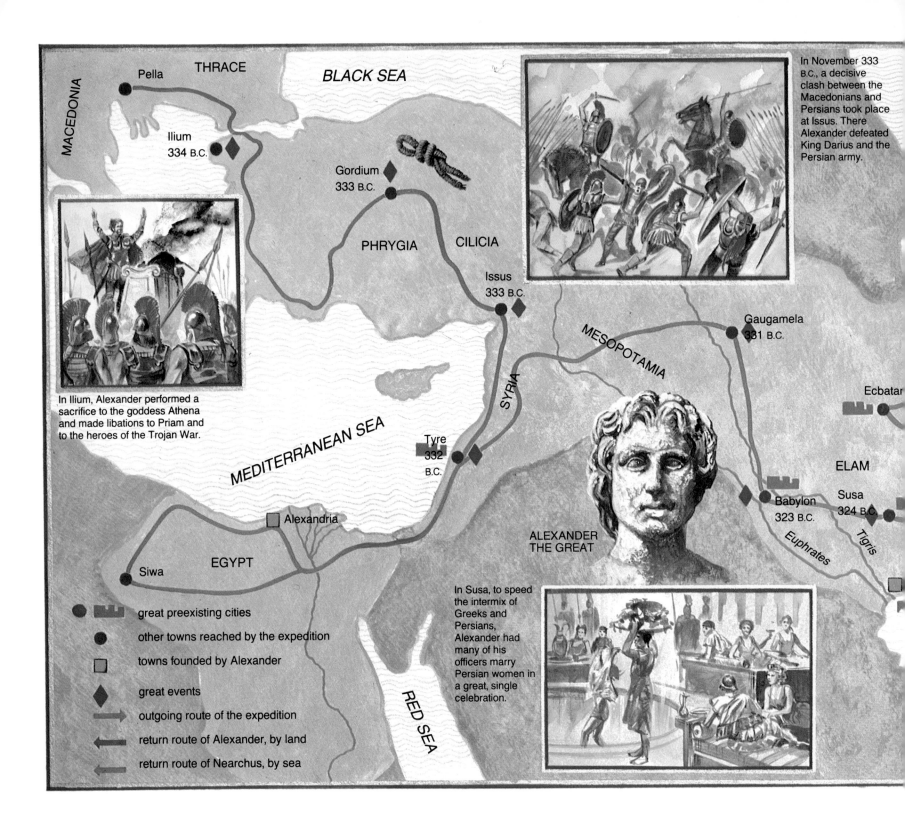

In Ilium, Alexander performed a sacrifice to the goddess Athena and made libations to Priam and to the heroes of the Trojan War.

In November 333 B.C., a decisive clash between the Macedonians and Persians took place at Issus. There Alexander defeated King Darius and the Persian army.

In Susa, to speed the intermix of Greeks and Persians, Alexander had many of his officers marry Persian women in a great, single celebration.

ALEXANDER THE GREAT

- ● ▬ great preexisting cities
- ● other towns reached by the expedition
- ▢ towns founded by Alexander
- ◆ great events
- ➡ outgoing route of the expedition
- ⬅ return route of Alexander, by land
- ⬅ return route of Nearchus, by sea

THE GREEKS CONQUER THE ORIENT

Alexander the Macedonian Avenges the Greeks

In the fourth century, the ancient hostility between Greeks and Persians burst into a new war. This war, however, would lead to the fall of Persia and the entire Achaemenid Empire. For in this war, the Persians faced not only the Greeks, but also the Macedonians led by Alexander the Great. Through his campaigns, Alex-

ander wished to get revenge on behalf of the Greeks, spread Hellenistic culture throughout the eastern regions, and strengthen the preexisting political alliances.

In 334 B.C., an army of about forty thousand men led by Alexander crossed the Hellespont and performed a sacrifice in Ilium in remembrance of the Trojan War. After a few months, almost all of Asia Minor had fallen into Alexander's hands. Alexander later penetrated Syria, where in the fall of 333 B.C., he defeated the Persian army led by the great commander Darius. With this victory, Alexander won access to the eastern coasts and Mesopotamia. The Phoenician towns were divided. Only Tyre

dared to resist the conquest and eventually had to surrender after a siege of seven months.

In Egypt, Alexander founded the city of Alexandria, and visited the oracle of Ammon in Siwa. From Egypt, Alexander made his way back to Asia. In October 331 B.C., at Gaugamela-Arbela, a decisive clash between Persians and Macedonians took place. Darius awaited Alexander on terrain which was favorable to his war chariots. But once again he was defeated and forced to flee the battlefield. The capitals of the empire now fell one after the other. Entering Babylon, Alexander offered a sacrifice to the god Marduk in order to become king of the entire world. In Persepolis, Alexander seized

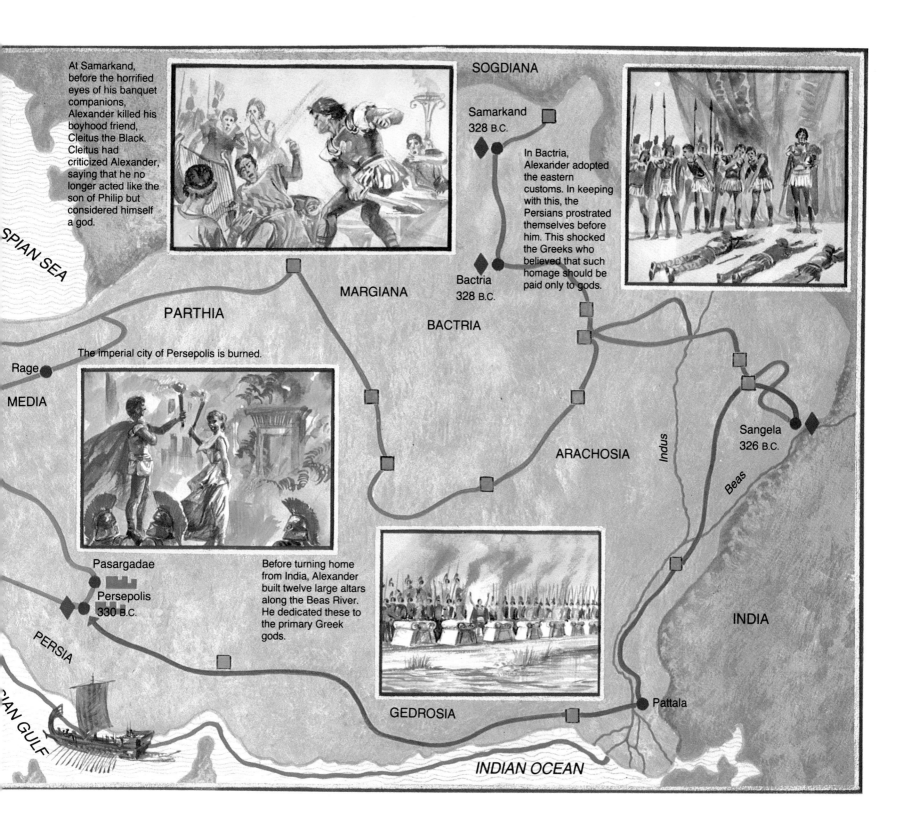

At Samarkand, before the horrified eyes of his banquet companions, Alexander killed his boyhood friend, Cleitus the Black. Cleitus had criticized Alexander, saying that he no longer acted like the son of Philip but considered himself a god.

SOGDIANA

Samarkand
328 B.C.

In Bactria, Alexander adopted the eastern customs. In keeping with this, the Persians prostrated themselves before him. This shocked the Greeks who believed that such homage should be paid only to gods.

Bactria
328 B.C.

SPIAN SEA

PARTHIA

MARGIANA

BACTRIA

The imperial city of Persepolis is burned.

Rage

MEDIA

ARACHOSIA

Indus

Sangela
326 B.C.

Beas

Pasargadae

Persepolis
330 B.C.

Before turning home from India, Alexander built twelve large altars along the Beas River. He dedicated these to the primary Greek gods.

INDIA

PERSIA

Pattala

GEDROSIA

IAN GULF

INDIAN OCEAN

the treasure of the Persian kings and burned the city. In the summer of 330 B.C., Darius was killed by Bessus, one of his own nobles. Alexander then proclaimed himself heir to the Achaemenid Empire.

The Conquest of the Orient

Alexander's army conquered Hyrcania, Parthia, Aria, Arachosia, and having passed the Hindu Kush, moved into Bactria and Sogdiana, where the plains of central Asia began. From Bactria, Alexander dreamed of reaching India, and headed in that direction. In 326 B.C., he allied himself with the king of Taxila against Porus, an Indian prince. Again victorious, he

crossed the Indus River and reached one of its tributaries, the Beas River. At this point, his soldiers refused to go any farther.

On the way back, the Macedonian army marched down the course of the Indus River for a time, then divided into two groups. Nearchus, one of Alexander's commanders, led the fleet by sea to the outlets of the Tigris and the Euphrates rivers. Alexander, with part of the army, took the more difficult way through the terrible desert of Gedrosia. The forces were rejoined in Susa.

After only a few years of war, the political ideas of Alexander had changed. He wished for the Greeks and the "barbarians" to mingle and to create a new political unity. To aid this

merger, Alexander encouraged mixed marriages. He himself married the daughter of a Sogdiana noble and later three Persian princesses. In Susa, numerous Greek generals and soldiers married "barbarian" women, all in a single day. For the capital city of this vast empire, Alexander chose Babylon. Returning to that city to reunite the army, Alexander suddenly fell sick with malaria. After a few days' struggle, Alexander died on June 13, 323 B.C.

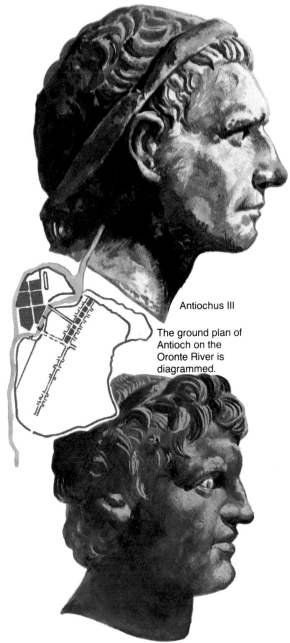

Antiochus III

The ground plan of Antioch on the Oronte River is diagrammed.

A bronze head of Seleucus I, the founder of the dynasty, is pictured.

The main road of Antioch was very wide, paved with stone slabs, and furnished with sidewalks. It was flanked by colonnades under which were numerous stores. Its population was composed of artisans, farmers, merchants, and slaves. Trade activities flourished. The way of life was similar to that of Greece. The camel was frequently used for the transportation of goods.

THE KINGDOM OF THE SELEUCIDS

The Birth of the Hellenistic States

Alexander died without an appointed heir. His generals, who considered themselves to be his successors, began to fight over the empire. Some of the generals wished to keep Alexander's empire united; others wanted to create independent states. In 321 B.C., the territories of the empire were assigned to the rule of various generals.

Many clashes among these generals occurred. Eventually, between 307 and 305 B.C., each general was given the title of king, and the empire was divided into separate kingdoms. Macedonia, including Greece, came under the rule of the dynasty of the Antigonids. Anatolia, Mesopotamia, Syria, and the Asian lands to the east passed into the hands of the Seleucids.

Egypt was ruled by the dynasty of the Ptolemies. In all of these states, the Greek conquerors continued to rule over the preexisting populations. These states came to be called Hellenistic states.

The Seleucids, Founders of Towns

The dynasty of the Seleucids was initiated by Seleucus I Nicator, who controlled the bulk of the empire. He succeeded the Great Kings of Persia. The Seleucids added an important feature to the traditional governmental system of the Persians. They built numerous fortified towns, sending Greeks and Macedonians to populate them. All of these towns had a high degree of independence, but they were protected by a royal garrison and were under the

This statue of the city deity, Athena Tyche, dates from the third century B.C. Representing the good luck of Antioch, she sits on a rock, her head crowned by fortified walls. At her feet is the Orontes River.

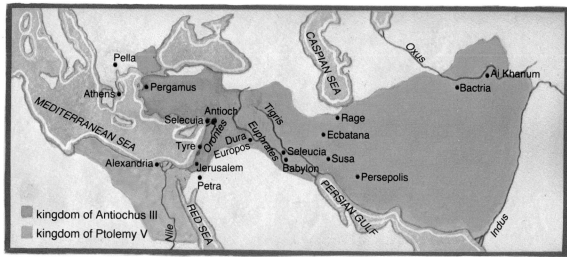

At its peak, the kingdom of the Seleucids covered a vast territory.

The main temple of Khanum was located in one of the Greek towns in Bactria. In the background is the morning mist rising from the river Oxus.

control of a governor. The towns of the Seleucids were great centers of Hellenistic culture. The most important of these was Antioch in Syria. Founded by Seleucus I on the Orontes River, this town became the kingdom's capital.

The economic life of the kingdom of the Seleucids was based on agricultural production and trade. The sovereigns took special care in maintaining the network of roads that served as trade routes. These roads went from India to the Mediterranean harbor towns.

The Loss of the East

The kingdom of the Seleucids was so vast that it was difficult to rule. By 303 B.C., the Indian territories had already been abandoned. Because of changes in the Seleucids' military, political, and economic interests in the Mediterranean, managing the central and eastern parts of the empire also became impossible.

In 239 B.C., Iranian populations from the steppes of central Asia invaded the territories along the Caspian Sea. These were the Parthians, against whom the Seleucids fought many wars. Gradually, the Parthians conquered many

regions of the empire. This resulted in a disruption of communication between the core of the Seleucid kingdom and its easternmost territories.

The eastern part of the empire showed increasing tendencies toward secession. At the end of the third century, the Seleucids were forced to recognize the independence of the kingdom of Bactria. This was a vast territory, stretching all the way to northwest India. Still other divisions followed. The Greek-Bactrian territories developed in their own direction and continued to spread Hellenistic culture toward central Asia and India. Eventually, in 100 B.C., they were conquered by the Scythians and later by the Kushans.

The End of the Seleucid Kingdom

The gradual loss of territories to the east, and constant fights with Egypt over Syria to the west, reduced the kingdom's military strength. King Antiochus III attempted to regain the territories that had been seized by the Parthians and backed Macedonia in the war against Rome (192-188 B.C.). But both the Parthians and the

Romans, who were already present on the eastern Mediterranean, were too powerful for the Seleucids. Upon the death of Antiochus III in 187 B.C., the dynasty declined rapidly.

Hellenistic Palestine

Initially, Palestine was ruled by the Ptolemies of Egypt. In 198 B.C. it was annexed to the kingdom of Antiochus III. Under Antiochus III, the Jews were allowed to continue their cultural and religious ways. When Antiochus IV came to power, however, he tried to force Greek culture on the Jews. Many of the Jews resisted.

The tension grew until it burst out into a war for independence. The Seleucids reacted harshly, and Antiochus IV had an altar for the god Zeus built in the Jews' Temple. The history of Judaism seemed close to its end until a movement of political opposition began led by a family of priests known as the Hasmoneans. In 164 B.C., one of these priests, Judas Maccabee, seized Jerusalem, purified and rededicated the Temple, and began a period of Hasmonean rule.

THE KINGDOM OF PERGAMUM

In Asia Minor, close to the Mediterranean, the small town of Pergamum became independent of the Seleucids in 263 B.C. At first its territory was very small, but it was located in a favorable position and was rather wealthy. The princes of Pergamum sought to expand their country, taking advantage of the constant fights which were weakening the Seleucids. Following military success, Attalus I became king, and by 189 B.C., most of the Seleucid territories belonged to Pergamum.

The rulers of the Attalid dynasty were excellent diplomats in the Mediterranean area. They realized that the small kingdom of Pergamum, squeezed between Macedonia in Europe and the Seleucids in Asia, could never survive without support from a major power. Thus they allied themselves with Rome and were able to expand their terrritory. They scored several victories against the Celtic populations who lived in northern Phrygia and often raided the kingdom.

The City of Pergamum

Under the Attalid dynasty, Pergamum became one of the most important cities of Hellenistic times. The site where the town had developed, however, was not the best suited for construction work. It was a steep rocky spur at the junction of two rivers. The architects who designed the plan for the city abandoned the classical scheme of Hellenistic towns where streets crossed at right angles. Instead, they used the terrain's natural features. Showing great skill in urban landscaping, they built a city on three levels interconnected by staircases. The upper city, the most monumental, was developed around a double square and contained a large altar to Zeus, a library, and a theater built on the slope of the rocky outcrop.

Pergamum was also a major cultural center, particularly under kings Attalus I and Eumemes

II when it matched the grandeur of Alexandria, Egypt. The city was the meeting point for literary scholars, philosophers, and artists. The extensive library, supported by the king's treasury, contained many works from the Greek culture.

An important technical achievement was the introduction of parchment, the name of which was derived from the name of the city. This writing material was invented to bypass the Egyptian monopoly on papyrus. Parchment was made from sheep or ram skin processed in a special way and made into a sturdy roll. This new material spread rapidly through the ancient world and was to be used even in Medieval Europe. Paper, invented in China almost at the same time, reached Europe much later.

Pergamum and Hellenistic Art

Some of the Hellenistic world's most significant artwork was produced in Pergamum. Two of them are reproduced on this page: a statue called the *Dying Gaul* and the altar of Zeus. The statue was part of a great circular monument built in memory of the defeat of the Galatians. The altar of Zeus is the most important monument of Hellenistic culture still in existence. It was built in 190 B.C. by Antiochus III to celebrate a military victory. Its imposing size was a mark of Hellenistic art.

The construction of colossal monuments was an expression of power and strength used by many kings in Hellenistic towns. Another feature of Hellenistic art was its realism, in both sculpting and painting. Great attention was paid to detail, features, and individual differences. The artists attempted to depict even the conditions of old age, sickness, sufferings, and ethnic differences. The great ideal themes of classical Greece were abandoned, and the favorite themes were scenes of daily life, still lifes, and landscapes.

Top: The kingdom of Pergamum at the Aegean borders of Asia in 240 (light pink) and 185 B.C. (dark pink) is mapped. *Bottom:* The plan of Pergamum with the acropolis (**1**) and the gymnasium (**2**) is diagrammed.

This statue called the *Dying Gaul* was part of a bronze group erected by King Attalus I (241-197 B.C.) in memory of his victories over the Galatians. This is one of the most notable statues of Hellenism. The respect paid to the defeated enemy is evident in this work of art.

Antiochus III built the altar to Zeus to celebrate the victory over the Galatians. It is the most important monument of Hellenistic art.

ram

stretched skin

tanned
roll

written parchment

The processing of parchment began in the city of
Pergamum.

The acropolis of Pergamum: **1)** Agora; **2)** altar to Zeus;
3) marketplace; **4)** theater; **5)** temple of Athena; **6)**
library, partially hidden by the colonnade of the temple
of Athena.

A coin bears the profile of Mithridates IV of Pontus.

The profile of Tigranes the Great is seen on the coin above.

Roman cavalryman

The sections above illustrate the Roman Expansion. **1)** The Battle of Magnesia, 190 B.C., is diagrammed. **2)** This drawing shows an example of the tactics of the Roman legions. Although sometimes weak in frontal attack, the Romans succeeded in attacking the flanks of enemy troops. **3)** Shaded areas represent the kingdoms of Pontus and Armenia. **(4)** This map shows Roman expansion in Asia.

THE ROMANS CONQUER THE EAST

Roman expansion into the eastern Mediterranean began on the Greek peninsula. The Romans had been called in to defend their allies on Italy's eastern coast. But once there, they took an offensive stance against the Macedonians in defense of the Greeks. In 196 B.C., the Romans proclaimed the liberty of the Greek cities.

By 200 B.C., Rome was on its way to becoming the strongest power in the Mediterranean, but the Seleucid Empire was still strong in Asia. The Seleucids were defeated at Thermopylae (191 B.C.), at Magnesia (190 B.C.), and were later forced to confine themselves to Syria.

Meanwhile, the kingdom of Pergamum, allied with the Romans, was enlarged. Shrewd Roman diplomacy toward the smaller kingdoms of Asia Minor rendered them all allies of Rome. Under Rome's protection, the Armenian rulers, both north and south, declared themselves independent of the Seleucids. The next step in the Roman expansion came when King Attalus III of the independent kingdom of Pergamum died in 133 B.C. Having no heir, Attalus willed the kingdom to the Romans. In this territory, Rome established the province of Asia Minor. Shortly afterward, Cilicia also became a province.

Armenia Under Tigranes the Great

Around 100 B.C., the Roman advance was gravely shaken by the expansion of Armenia and by the resistance of Mithridates, the king of Pontus. Armenia, having been divided into two principalities, had been exposed to attacks by

People stream into the Temple of Jerusalem, which Herod the Great had rebuilt.

the Parthians. Under Tigranes the Great, however, Armenia unified and expanded. Tigranes seized control of a Parthian province and eventually reached Mesopotamia.

In 83 B.C., some Greek cities, especially Antioch, called upon Tigranes to be the successor to the Seleucids. Tigranes' Armenian Empire thus extended from the Caspian Sea to the Mediterranean Sea. It lasted a short time but permitted Tigranes to spread Hellenization. He transferred the Greek population and created cities in the center of Armenia.

Mithridates Challenges the Romans

Farther west, situated on the Black Sea, the kingdom of Pontus gained strength in these same years. Under King Mithridates Eupator, it took to the field against the Romans. In the first war (89-85 B.C.), Mithridates occupied Rome's allied kingdoms of Bithynia and Cappadocia, then invaded Roman Asia. All of anti-Roman Greece fought with him. The Roman leader Sulla repelled Mithridates from Asia and forced him to make peace.

With the second war, Mithridates was chased from Cappadocia (83-81 B.C.). With the third war (74-65 B.C.), the Romans won a decisive victory. To prepare himself for this great conflict, Mithridates had allied himself with Tigranes, the Armenian king, and had gathered an army. The Roman victory, primed by General Lucullus, was completed by Pompey the Great in 66 B.C. Mithridates committed suicide. Armenia, thus defeated, returned to being a Roman protectorate and was to remain a buffer zone between Rome and the Parthians for more than a century.

Conquest of the Hasmonean Kingdom of Palestine

Under John Hyrcanus (134-104 B.C.), one of the Hasmonean leaders after Judas Maccabee, the Hasmonean kingdom extended itself from the confines of Judaea into a territory equal in size to the kingdom of David. But soon after, began to decline, enmeshed in internal struggles. Rule of the Palestinian kingdom had fallen to two brothers, Aristobolus II and Hyrcanus II. The brothers turned to Pompey, who was at that time residing in Damascus. In 63 B.C., Pompey put Aristobolus at the head of Jerusalem and victoriously entered the city and its Temple. There he named Hyrcanus II as high priest, but Palestine was reduced to little more than a Roman satellite. Under the reign of Herod, a Roman vassal, the Temple was practically rebuilt between 20 and 10 B.C.

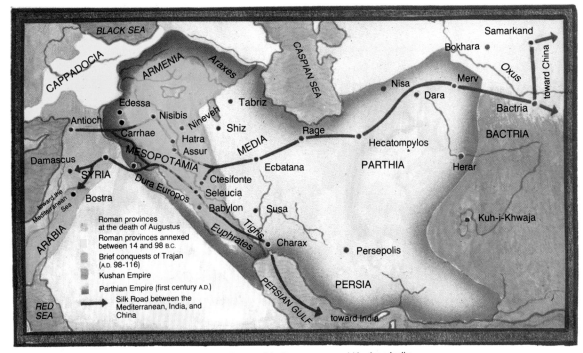

The Parthian Empire was situated between the Roman Mediterranean and Kushan India.

THE PARTHIAN EMPIRE

Around 250 B.C., nomads of Iranian heritage descended from the Orient and pushed into the territory south of the Caspian Sea. There they conquered Parthia, taking it from the Seleucid Empire, and proclaimed Arsaces, one of their own chiefs, king. From the area of their initial conquests, the Parthians, as they were called, extended themselves throughout other territories in Iran. In 141 B.C., the Parthian king Mithridates I gained control of Seleucia, the great Seleucid city on the Tigris River, and proclaimed himself king of Babylon.

Conflict Over the Euphrates

Under the reign of Mithridates II (from around 123 B.C.), the Parthian Empire nearly became a worldwide power. The influence of Rome, however, was spreading outward from the Mediterranean in the opposite direction. The Euphrates River was to be, for centuries, a point of conflict between these two empires struggling for control of the Middle East.

The Roman leader Crassus, seeking a glorious victory in the east, led an expedition against the Parthians, but was disastrously defeated in the Battle of Carrhae (53 B.C.). Crassus lost his life, as did many of his soldiers, and the Parthians captured the insignia of the Roman legions. Some thirty years later, in 20 B.C., the Roman emperor Augustus sought to make peace. With a treaty, Augustus obtained the return of Roman prisoners and the insignias.

But a century later, the Roman emperor Trajan resumed hostilities and succeeded in conquering southern Arabia, Armenia, Mesopota-

This statue is of a Parthian warrior in the uniform of a commander, from Hatra, second century A.D.

A Parthian king grants power to a provincial governor, giving him a crown.

Combat Techniques

Parthian combat methods disrupted the orderly Roman legions. The Parthians were skilled horsemen and excellent archers. They struck effectively and then rapidly retreated, protecting themselves with arrows. The "Parthian shot," as it was called, launched by an invincibly quick horseman, became famous. Toward the end of the Parthian epoch, heavy cavalry appeared, as shown in drawings from the period of armored cavalrymen.

In a fresco from Dura Europos (first century A.D.), three people offer a sacrifice to the god Bel. The figures in the fresco are characteristic of Parthian art.

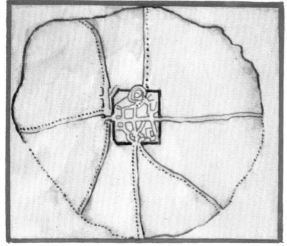

This plan was drawn for the city of Merv, which was the most important city of the region of Margiana. The city's enclosed center remained from the Seleucid Empire and followed the model of Greek urban planning. The Parthians used it as the new city's center and added circular walls for defense.

This head belongs to a colossal statue dedicated to the god Apollo-Mitra. It was found, together with others, among the ruins of the funerary mound of Antiochus I Commagenes at Nimrud-Dag in southern Anatolia. It dates from the first century B.C.

mia, and Babylonia. Hadrian, his successor, changed his policy toward the Orient. He restored these territories to the Parthians, making the Euphrates River the boundary once again.

The Parthians and the Steppe Populations

For the Parthian Empire, the situation was more complicated to the north and east. In these regions, there was great fear of Iranian nomadic tribes. These tribes were pushing from the steppe and from the passes of the Caucasus.

Across the borders with India, the power of the Kushan Empire was growing. After having taken the Greek states of Bactria, the Kushans created a vast empire which included the Indus Valley and stretched to the Ganges Valley. The Parthians, attracted more to the west than to the east, tried to avoid disagreements with the Kushans.

The government of the Parthian Empire maintained the established systems. The ap-

pointment of governors, or satraps, came from the noble Achaemenid families; the organization of cities followed the Hellenistic tradition. The kings owned a considerable portion of the land, and governed the country through the nobility. The nobility was made up either of officers or of local princes who possessed their own armies.

The empire grew wealthy because of many merchant caravans that crossed it. One particularly important travel route had developed when the Mediterranean, under Roman rule, had become a great market and when faraway China had been unified under the Han dynasty. The so-called Silk Road carried that precious and highly prized product to the west.

Architecture and Art

The few Parthian cities were built with a circular plan typical of the nomadic encampments. In their building techniques, the Parthians returned to and renewed the Iranian architectural tradition. In time, terraces were replaced with vaulted roofs introduced by eastern Iran. The central chamber had three enclosed walls, a barrel vault, and instead of the fourth wall, an opening toward the east. This room was the ivan, which may have resembled a tent.

The Parthians kept the religious and cultural traditions of the steppe nomads but were greatly attracted to Hellenism. Until around the first century A.D., the Arsacidae dynasty (the ruling dynasty begun by Arsaces) encouraged Hellenization. One example of this Hellenization is the funeral monument to Antiochus I Commagenes at Nimrud-Dag (from the first century A.D.). On this monument, the gods are depicted in the Greek mode. Before this, the Iranians had never depicted divinity in human form.

THE LIFE AND TEACHINGS OF JESUS CHRIST

During the reign of Herod in Palestine—then effectively under Roman control—something unforseen occurred. This event, the birth of Jesus Christ, changed the history of the Hebrew people and the lives of many peoples and lands.

Jesus Christ, a descendant of King David, was born in the city of Bethlehem in Judaea. When Jesus was presented at the Temple for circumcision, which was a common ritual among the Jews, two pious Israelites, Simeon and Anne, announced that the baby would become the Messiah. The Messiah was the descendant of David who, according to predictions and scripture, would free the Jewish people. Until his thirtieth year, Jesus lived at Nazareth, in Galilee.

The Beginning of Jesus' Public Life

In A.D. 28-29, the prophet John the Baptist began to preach along the River Jordan. In his teachings, John urged the Jews to live lives of virtue, justice, and truth. Along the way, John baptized many people in the Jordan, including Jesus.

After a period of fasting in the desert, Jesus started to preach. His goal was to proclaim the Kingdom of God. Jesus wanted to show the people that God was not an incomprehensible power but was the Father of all. In doing this, Jesus spoke to the humble, the simple, and the sick. He also knew the art of healing and cured the lame, the blind, and the leprous.

Jesus had many followers. People were awed by his great humanity, by his capacity to understand and care for everyone he met, by his powerful speech, and by his goodness. From among these followers, Jesus chose twelve men to be his disciples and assist him. These men were called apostles.

The Passion

Jesus' arrival alarmed the two most powerful groups of Jews: the Pharisees and the Sadducees. The Pharisees feared that Jesus' teachings would change the religious practices. The Sadducees feared that Jesus' popularity would lead to possible political disorder. Some of his followers, including the apostles, insisted that Jesus had come to free Israel from the Roman Empire.

In the spring of A.D. 30 or 33, Jesus arrived in Jerusalem to celebrate the Passover, the Jewish

Accompanied by his disciples, Jesus preaches to the people.

festival celebrating their liberation from Egypt. Jesus was welcomed by the people of the city, who saluted him as their king, the Messiah. He preached in the Temple and celebrated with his disciples.

Betrayed by one of his disciples, Judas, Jesus was arrested and taken before the Jewish high priests. These leaders questioned him, asking him if he was the Son of God. When Jesus did not deny this, the leaders accused him of having blasphemed. They then took him to Pontius Pilate, the Roman governor. The high priests told Pilate that Jesus had claimed he was the King of the Jews. At their urging, Pilate sentenced Jesus to death by crucifixion.

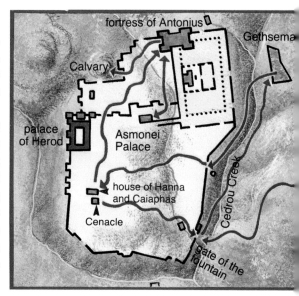

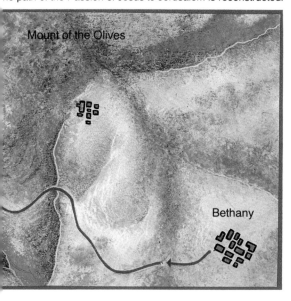

The path of the Passion of Jesus to Jerusalem is reconstructed.

Mount of the Olives

Bethany

The Resurrection

Christians believe that Jesus rose from the dead three days after his crucifixion. The celebration of his resurrection is known as Easter Sunday. Knowledge of the resurrection comes from the testimony of Jesus' disciples as recorded in the Gospels. Doubtful at first, the apostles themselves were convinced of the event only through meetings with the resurrected Christ. The Gospels tell how one of Jesus' followers, Mary Magdalene, discovered his empty tomb. The writings also relate several appearances of Jesus to the apostles and his ascension into heaven. These events constitute the foundation of the Christian religion.

The New Testament

The texts of the Bible that narrate Jesus' life and the beginning of the Christian community are called the New Testament. Jesus did not record his own teachings. These, like the story of his life, were later written down by his disciples. Nearly all knowledge of Jesus' life comes from four short books within the New Testament. The books are called the Gospels, which means "good news." They were written by Matthew, Mark, Luke, and John.

Other writings of the New Testament include the Acts of the Apostles and the Epistles (letters). In the Acts of the Apostles, Luke recounts the deeds of the first Christian community through the arrival of Paul in Rome. Tradition attributes fourteen of these letters to Paul. Scholars are certain that Paul wrote five or six of these but recognize that the others may not have been his work. Three other letters, as well as the Apocalypse, are attributed to the apostle John. Finally, two were written by Peter, one by Jacob, and one by Judah. All of these texts were written in the second half of the first century A.D.

The round plaza in Gerasa, characterized by four groups of four columns each, was built in the third century A.D.

THE EASTERN EMPERORS AND ROMANIZATION

Asia was a land of ancient civilizations which had already seen a great deal of political organization and urban life. The Romans undertook the task of ruling this greatly refined world with respect and caution. After gaining control of the territory, they became tolerant of local customs. They allowed the Greek towns to retain formal freedom and, especially from the second century A.D. on, they encouraged people from the eastern regions to become members of the senate and of the government of the empire.

This effort was well rewarded. It helped to merge the eastern Hellenistic traditions and the Roman traditions. People from the east were at ease in the empire. Even when the western part of the empire was lost to the barbarians, the east remained faithful to Rome.

The political integration of the Orient with Rome reached its height in the third century. At that time, Julia Domna, who belonged to the royal dynasty of the priests of the sun god of Emesa, in Syria, married Septimius Severus, who became the Roman emperor. Their offspring, from Caracall to Severus Alexander, were to rule the empire (A.D. 211-235). Later on, Philip the Arabian became emperor. Of Arabian descent, Philip was considered by many to be the first Christian emperor.

Philip II the Arab

Cultural Exchanges

The Romans were true protectors of Hellenism. They so admired it that they invited masters of the Greek culture to come to Italy. They also brought large quantities of artwork from the Orient to decorate their towns and homes. This artistic and cultural influx greatly transformed the Roman world, making it more refined. Thanks to these exchanges, some Greek thought, such as Stoicism, found an outlet in Rome.

Despite Roman influence, the original Hellenistic culture continued vigorously. The Greek language remained predominant, but beginning in the third century, local languages began to reappear. In the fine arts, especially in architecture, Roman patterns and styles were used side by side with those from the Orient. As seen in the great monuments of Petra, Gerasa, Palmira,

The city of Miletus probably look similar to this in the Roman epoch.

Miletus

Rodhus

MEDITERRANEAN SEA

Antioch

Palmira

Baalbek

Berytos

Gerasa

Petra

Left: Remains of the arch and column-flanked road in Palmira are seen. This ancient oasis in the Syrian Desert reached its spendor in the third century A.D. in the Roman epoch.

To the right, top: The central court in the acropolis of Baalbek is seen in detail. The acropolis was a large Roman architectural complex. *Lower right:* The remains of a tomb stand on the side of the ancient city of Petra, the well-known caravan town. The Romans made this city into an Arabic province in A.D. 106.

The archaeological remains of the temple of Mithras were found in Dura Europos.

The map shows some of the important Asian cities of the Roman Empire.

The Cult of Mithras

Mithras, god of the sun, was of Iranian origin. Mithras was the protector god of the Parthian sovereigns, and the soldiers of the Roman army spread the cult from Mesopotamia to all of the provinces of the Roman Empire.

According to mythology, the sun ordered Mithras to kill the primeval bull. Sadly, Mithras obeyed. The bull's death set the creation of the world in motion. After the task was complete, Mithras and the sun feasted. This feast became a model for ritual meals of the faithful.

Mithras was honored by the emperors of the third century A.D., especially Aurelianus. Worship was done in Latin, and there were various degrees of participation. Special ceremonies marked the passage from one level to the next.

and Baalbek, the proportions of the buildings changed. Straight lines gave way to interrupted ones, and curved surfaces appeared.

Within the Roman Empire, the Orient stood out for its incredible wealth. The level of prosperity experienced in these territories, Syria in particular, remained unmatched. Through the Silk Road, precious fabric was brought to the Mediterranean coast. Silk fabric had been developed in China, which held a monopoly over it. This fabric was highly sought after in Rome since its appearance at the beginning of the Christian Era. Besides trade, other major factors which contributed to the development and well-being of the eastern territories were a density of industrious peoples and the use of specialized agriculture.

The Explosion of Religions

Great forms of religious expression had developed in the Orient. Rome was very influenced by them since the period of the Republic. When Christianity spread throughout the Orient, it stimulated the pre-existing religions to new growth. This sudden religious fervor was the result of the general desire for salvation which was rapidly arising in the minds of the people. Within a short period of time, the Orient became a vital religious center. This vitality seeped into Italy and into the western part of the empire, mainly through the army. Priests and the faithful belonging to the most diverse cults were found throughout the territory. Among the most important cults was that of Mithras, god of the sun.

Hunting was one of the favorite sports of Sassanian sovereigns and nobles. In the illustration, a group of Sassanians hunt boar in a swamp.

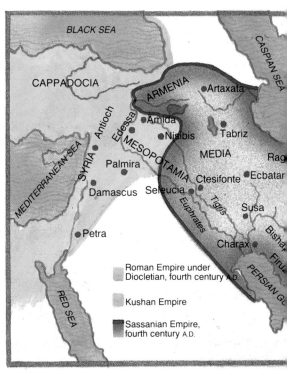

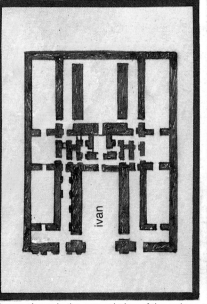

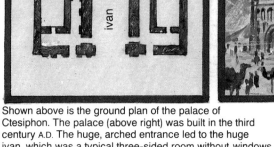

Shown above is the ground plan of the palace of Ctesiphon. The palace (above right) was built in the third century A.D. The huge, arched entrance led to the huge ivan, which was a typical three-sided room without windows.

THE SASSANIANS

The kingdom of the Parthians was shaken by violent internal conflicts during the last years of its existence. In A.D. 227 Ardashir, prince of the small province of Perside, collected all of his forces and defeated the last king of the Parthian dynasty. The new sovereigns were called Sassanians after Ardashir's grandfather, Sassan. The Sassanians came from a region in the heart of Iran and appeared to be the restorers of the national and religious traditions.

The Sassanians, as had been the case with the Parthians, were kept busy defending their territory. To the east, the new sovereigns had to deal with the steppe populations; to the west the Roman Empire was a source of trouble. But the Sassanians were not willing to give up any territory to Rome. In fact, they conquered some Roman land and established the border between the two empires along the Euphrates River.

Wars among Romans and Sassanians were frequent in the third century. A catastrophic fight for the Romans occurred between the Sassanian king Shapur I and the Roman emperor Valerian. Valerian was defeated and taken prisoner in A.D. 260.

The Society

A real Sassanian innovation was the reorganization of the government. Under the sovereign, officials were responsible for individual provinces. This system made it possible to keep the country united. Additionally, people from all social classes served in the army. The nobles formed the armored cavalry, farmers formed the attack platoons, and skilled auxiliary soldiers were hired from bordering nations.

In social life, the importance of the nobility increased. This was due to the fact that the

sovereigns, to avoid being controlled by the ancient noble Achaemenid families, constantly created new nobles. The Sassanian society can be imagined as a series of concentric circles. At the center was the king with his court, followed by the great families of the Achaemenid tradition. Next came the lords and the nobles who had reached this status in recent times, followed by the small noble landowners. These landowners, also called free men, had the task of collecting taxes in their territory. Finally, in the last circle were farmers and shepherds.

Religion

Under the Sassanians, Zoroaster's religion, Zoroastrianism, became the state religion. The Magi, an ancient caste of priests who performed the sacrifices, also accepted the doctrine of Zoroaster. However, the Sassanian Empire was

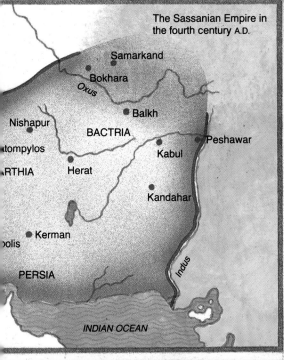

Samarkand

Bokhara
Oxus
Balkh

Nishapur
BACTRIA
Peshawar

tompylos
Kabul

RTHIA
Herat

Kandahar

Kerman
olis

PERSIA
Indus

INDIAN OCEAN

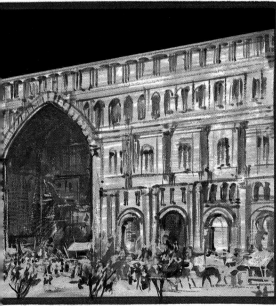

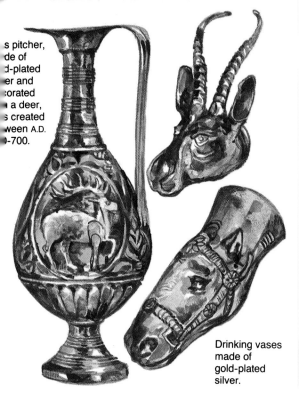

s pitcher, de of d-plated er and corated a deer, s created ween A.D. -700.

Drinking vases made of gold-plated silver.

The Sassanian king Shapur I accepts the surrender of a Roman emperor. The illustration is taken from a rock bas-relief in Naqsh-i-Rustam, from the third century A.D.

Mani and Manicheism

Mani was a great religious figure. He was born in Ctesiphon in A.D. 216, and grew up in an environment of Judaic-Christian fervor. He experienced two divine revelations, knew Indian spirituality, and for a certain period was allowed to preach in public. But during the rule of Sassanian king Bahram I, the Magi accused Mani of drawing the people away from the official religion. Under pressure from this group, the king sentenced Mani to death. Mani died after twenty-six days of suffering.

The basic principles of Manicheism are contained in a book written by Mani himself. Through them, Manicheism offered a path to salvation. It preached that God was the highest good and that creation was the work of the Prince of Darkness who sought to gain possession of the light of God. Human beings have light within them, but this light is imprisoned inside the bodily matter. Through knowledge, it is possible to escape from the prison of life, nature, and existence, thus returning the light to God and destroying the world. This religious ideal believed in a final victory for God, at the expense of life, nature, the world, and the body, all of which were considered expressions of evil.

not exempt from the influence of religions that were typical of the east at this time. Other cults, such as that of fire, continued to be followed, and new religions were introduced.

The Art

In Ctesiphon, a town of Parthian origin, Shapur I built a magnificent palace. At the front of the palace, was an ivan, which was a huge, three-sided, windowless room. The fourth side opened to the outside through a pointed arch.

The Sassanians learned a great deal about urban planning from Roman prisoners and from other foreign workers who were called to build the Sassanian towns. They would often abandon the traditional circular plan of the Parthian towns, replacing it with Hellenistic plans that arranged streets at right angles.

A typical form of Sassanian art was the bas-relief stone sculpture. Sovereigns used sculpture to celebrate their dynasty and their military victories. A little later, the Sassanians' skill in reproducing human and animal shapes was expressed in jewelry, in patterns on fabric, and in objects of daily use.

The apostle
Paul

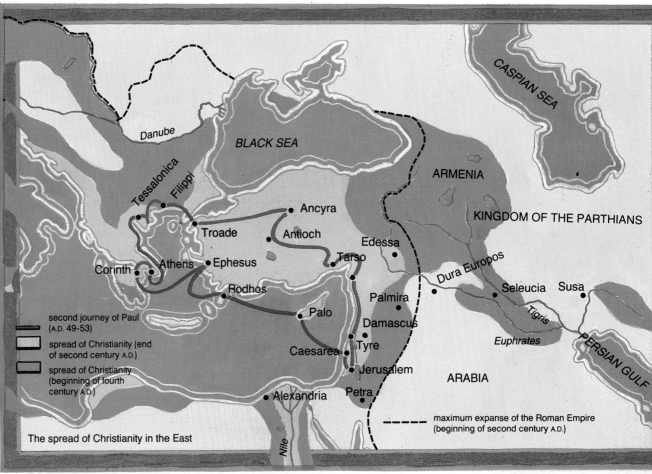

second journey of Paul
(A.D. 49-53)

spread of Christianity (end
of second century A.D.)

spread of Christianity
(beginning of fourth
century A.D.)

maximum expanse of the Roman Empire
(beginning of second century A.D.)

The spread of Christianity in the East

Above is an illustration of the christening chapel of Dura Europos on the Euphrates River.
It is the most ancient Christian church known and was built at the end of the third century.

CHRISTIANITY IN THE ORIENT

The name *christianoi* appeared for the first time among the pagans of Antioch. The word indicated the followers of the new faith—the first of which were Jews. In the first Christian communities, people shared their possessions, lived a life of intense prayer, and met in private homes. Soon the Jews questioned whether it was possible for non-Jews (called Gentiles) to share in the Christian communities. In the Council of Jerusalem, the apostles Peter and Paul confronted each other on this issue. Paul's view that Gentiles could be converted to the new religion was accepted as correct. This decision permitted the spread of Christianity throughout the world.

Paul was a Jew who had converted to Christianity. He became very active in missionary work and contributed greatly to the early spread of Christianity. He preached mainly to Gentiles. Paul believed that Christianity was a religion for all human beings, and therefore nobody had the right to limit its spread. In his four journeys, Paul reached Syria and the coastal towns of Asia Minor, Macedonia, and Greece. In many towns, his preaching resulted in the formation of Christian communities, with which

Paul kept in touch by letter. In his last journey, Paul traveled to Rome, where he preached for two years. According to tradition, he died with Peter during the persecution of Nero in A.D. 67.

The Spread of Christianity

Toward the end of the second century A.D., Christianity began to spread throughout the Mediterranean region and blossomed in the eastern regions. The persecutions of the second century did not seriously hinder this expansion. In the third century, the periods of peace became longer, and when a general crisis struck the Roman Empire, the Christians' beliefs

proved much stronger than the beliefs of other cults and religions in the east.

The Church began to organize itself. Bishops were appointed to supervise the local religious leaders, or clergy. Special sites for religious celebration were built, and Christianity spread beyond the empire's borders. It was brought to Persia by isolated missionaries and later by the war prisoners of the Sassanian kings.

Christianity Faces the Greek Culture

In the Middle East, Christianity soon confronted Greek philosophical thought. To pagan

A group of missionaries visits some Christians in a Syrian village.

The apostle Peter

The Domus Ecclesia was found in Capharnaus. It was a house where the first Christians of the area would gather.

The Judaic War

In the first century, the political situation in Palestine worsened. Bad leadership had exasperated the population. Among the Jews were the Zealots. The Zealots wanted to use force to free the Jews from tyranny. In A.D. 66, war broke out. The Romans, at first expelled, slowly regained territory under the guidance of Vespasian and his son, Titus.

In the spring of A.D. 70, the final siege of Jerusalem began. It lasted for five months, with great sufferings on the part of the people now tyrannized by the Zealots. The Temple, which was also a fortress, was eventually set on fire and destroyed on August 6, A.D. 70. In September, the city was razed, and the Jewish people were sold as slaves.

At this point, the paths of Judaism and Christianity divided. With the destruction of the Temple, the Jews were deprived of the sacrificial site. They were left with only prayer and religious education. Their hopes for an apocalypse and the coming of a Messiah remained unfulfilled, and the teaching of the Pharisees became predominant.

thinkers, ideas such as revelation, incarnation, and the existence of a creator God were inconceivable. This prompted numerous attacks on Christianity. Christian writers called Apologists tried to defend the new religion and explain the Christian viewpoint. Some writers considered the Greek culture to be unimportant because it was connected to paganism. Others showed that Christianity could complete and enlarge the pagan culture.

The debate continued through the second and third centuries. The more the Christians tried to explain the novelty of Christ's message, the more they blended in the Greek philosophy.

This philosophy offered great possibilities for further investigation. It also used a language which was understood by all the human beings of the time.

The Hellenistic world teemed with religions, cults, and teachings which greatly influenced Christians. All of these currents are referred to by the name of *gnosis,* a Greek word meaning "knowledge." The Gnostics believed that the world was dominated by evil forces and that the human body was composed of evil matter, in which a spark of divine light had been imprisoned. This spark could be freed or saved only through knowledge.

The gnostic doctrine often presented itself as the true message of Christ. Supposedly, it had been secretly revealed to the disciples and passed on by them to a few chosen people. This meant that the message of salvation for everybody was lost, together with the positive concept of humans and the world. In the third century, the Gnostic current lost much of its strength, while the Christian churches were able to reaffirm their positive vision of the world. This trend was confirmed in A.D. 313, when Emperor Constantine granted peace to the Church throughout the Roman Empire.

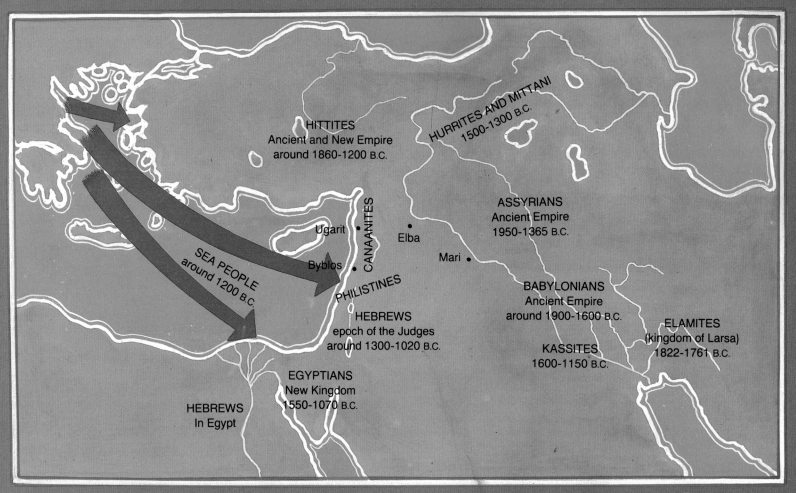

HITTITES
Ancient and New Empire
around 1860-1200 B.C.

HURRITES AND MITTANI
1500-1300 B.C.

ASSYRIANS
Ancient Empire
1950-1365 B.C.

Ugarit

CANAANITES

Elba

Mari

SEA PEOPLE
around 1200 B.C.

Byblos

PHILISTINES

BABYLONIANS
Ancient Empire
around 1900-1600 B.C.

ELAMITES
(kingdom of Larsa)
1822-1761 B.C.

HEBREWS
epoch of the Judges
around 1300-1020 B.C.

KASSITES
1600-1150 B.C.

EGYPTIANS
New Kingdom
1550-1070 B.C.

HEBREWS
In Egypt

The blossoming of Babylonians and Hittites occurred around 2000-1200 B.C.

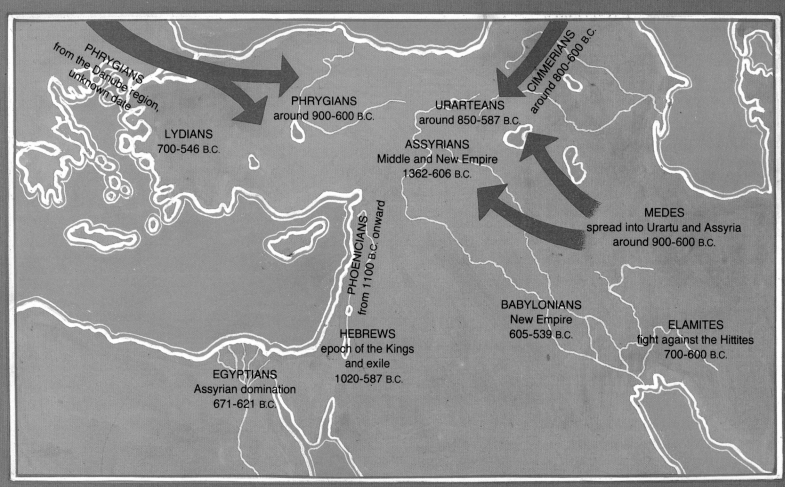

PHRYGIANS
from the Danube region,
unknown date

CIMMERIANS
around 800-600 B.C.

PHRYGIANS
around 900-600 B.C.

URARTEANS
around 850-587 B.C.

LYDIANS
700-546 B.C.

ASSYRIANS
Middle and New Empire
1362-606 B.C.

PHOENICIANS
from 1100 B.C. onward

MEDES
spread into Urartu and Assyria
around 900-600 B.C.

BABYLONIANS
New Empire
605-539 B.C.

ELAMITES
fight against the Hittites
700-600 B.C.

HEBREWS
epoch of the Kings
and exile
1020-587 B.C.

EGYPTIANS
Assyrian domination
671-621 B.C.

The deeds of Assyrians and Neobabylonians (around 1100-539 B.C.) are located above.

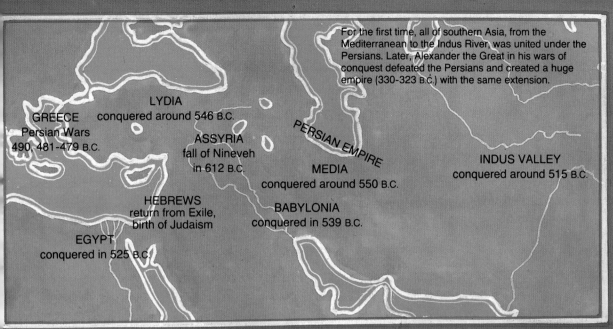

For the first time, all of southern Asia, from the Mediterranean to the Indus River, was united under the Persians. Later, Alexander the Great in his wars of conquest defeated the Persians and created a huge empire (330-323 B.C.) with the same extension.

GREECE
Persian Wars
490, 481-479 B.C.

LYDIA
conquered around 546 B.C.

ASSYRIA
fall of Nineveh
in 612 B.C.

PERSIAN EMPIRE

MEDIA
conquered around 550 B.C.

INDUS VALLEY
conquered around 515 B.C.

HEBREWS
return from Exile,
birth of Judaism

BABYLONIA
conquered in 539 B.C.

EGYPT
conquered in 525 B.C.

The Persian Empire and the Persian conquests around 600-330 B.C. are mapped.

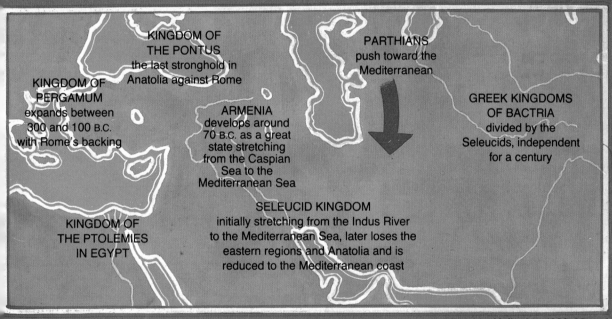

KINGDOM OF
THE PONTUS
the last stronghold in
Anatolia against Rome

PARTHIANS
push toward the
Mediterranean

KINGDOM OF
PERGAMUM
expands between
300 and 100 B.C.
with Rome's backing

ARMENIA
develops around
70 B.C. as a great
state stretching
from the Caspian
Sea to the
Mediterranean Sea

GREEK KINGDOMS
OF BACTRIA
divided by the
Seleucids, independent
for a century

KINGDOM OF
THE PTOLEMIES
IN EGYPT

SELEUCID KINGDOM
initially stretching from the Indus River
to the Mediterranean Sea, later loses the
eastern regions and Anatolia and is
reduced to the Mediterranean coast

Hellenism (323-63 B.C.)

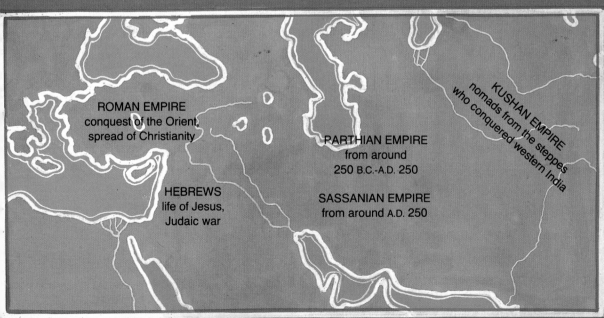

ROMAN EMPIRE
conquest of the Orient,
spread of Christianity

PARTHIAN EMPIRE
from around
250 B.C.-A.D. 250

KUSHAN EMPIRE
nomads from the steppes
who conquered western India

HEBREWS
life of Jesus,
Judaic war

SASSANIAN EMPIRE
from around A.D. 250

Roman, Parthian, and Sassanian empires (63 B.C.-around A.D. 300)

GLOSSARY

abolish: to do away with or destroy; to get rid of.

adaptation: change or adjustment by which a species or individual improves its condition in relationship to its environment. Animals or plants may change in physical form or behavior in order to live more efficiently in their habitat.

agriculture: the processes and activities associated with farming; the work of planting seeds, producing crops, and raising animals.

animal husbandry: an occupation which involves breeding and caring for domesticated animals.

architecture: the process or profession of designing buildings of all types.

archive: a special building or place where public records and official documents are housed.

arid: dry; devoid of moisture or humidity.

aristocracy: an elite class of people who are usually rich and powerful.

artifact: any object made or crafted by human hands.

artisan: a skilled craftsperson. The ancient artisans of the Middle East were highly imaginative.

astronomy: the study of the stars and planets.

Avesta: the sacred religious texts of the ancient Persians.

bas-relief: a piece of sculpture in which the figures are just barely raised from a flat background.

caravan: a group of people traveling together through a desert.

catastrophe: a terrible or terrifying occurrence; a tragedy or disaster.

cavalry: fighter troops which are either mounted on horses or transported in motorized vehicles.

ceramics: objects made of clay that are molded into shape and baked in an oven.

chalice: a cup or goblet, frequently used in religious rites or ceremonies.

citadel: a fortress or place of safety.

commerce: the process of buying, selling, and trading goods between one group or community and another.

conservation: the controlled use and protection of natural resources, such as forests and waterways.

continent: one of the principal land masses of the earth. Africa, Antarctica, Asia, Europe, North America, South America, and Australia are regarded as continents.

cult: a specific type of religious worship, attended by its own particular rules and ceremonies.

cultivate: to prepare land for the planting and growing of crops.

cuneiform: wedge-shaped symbols used in ancient Akkadian and Sumerian inscriptions.

deity: a god; a being who possesses a divine nature.

domesticate: the process of taming wild animals and then using them for different purposes.

dromedary: a camel with one hump. Dromedaries are used for transportation in the desert.

dynasty: a family of rulers; the period of time during which a specific family is in power. Zoser was the founder of Egypt's third dynasty.

edict: an official rule or proclamation.

emigrate: to leave one country or environment in order to settle in another.

ensi: during the Sumerian period, men who were priests as well as princes.

environment: the circumstances or conditions of a plant or animal's surroundings. The physical and social conditions of an organism's environment influence its growth and development.

epic: a long, narrative poem which relates heroic adventures or tales of a great nation.

epilogue: a final segment or closing speech added to the natural end of a book or play, which helps to provide further information or analysis.

epoch: the beginning of a new and important period in history.

evolution: a gradual process in which something changes into a different and usually more complex or better form. Groups of organisms may change with the passage of time so that descendants differ physically from their ancestors.

excavate: to make a hole or cavity in by digging; to form by hollowing out; to uncover or expose by digging.

expedition: a journey or exploratory mission undertaken in order to achieve a specific purpose.

fertile: rich in natural resources; able to produce or reproduce.

frieze: decorations placed to form a border around a room or building.

hostile: having the qualities or characteristics of any enemy; unfriendly.

hypothesis: a theory based on available supporting evidence.

immigrate: to move into a new region or country.

infantry: soldiers who are trained to fight on foot; foot soldiers.

irrigation: to carry or deliver water to dry land by artificial means such as tunnels or ditches.

kaunakes: short skirts made of fur or sheep's wool, which were the common clothes of the ancient Sumerians.

lance: a spear-shaped weapon.

lapis lazuli: a blue gemstone highly prized for jewelry and armor in ancient times.

liberate: to set free or release from bondage.

lunar: having to do with the moon and its changing phases.

lute: a stringed instrument much like a guitar which was used in ancient times.

lyre: a small harplike instrument used in ancient cultures to provide musical entertainment.

Mesopotamia: an ancient country in Southwest Asia which was between the Tigris and Euphrates rivers. Modern-day Iraq covers part of ancient Mesopotamia.

migrate: to move from place to place in search of food and shelter. Migration usually revolves around seasonal changes.

mollusk: any of a large group of animals having soft bodies enclosed in hard shells. Snails, oysters, and clams are mollusks.

monarch: the primary ruler of a state or kingdom, such as a king or queen.

Nebuchadnezzar: a Neobabylonian king (605-562 B.C.). The reign of Nebuchadnezzar marked the period of highest splendor of the Neobabylonian empire.

nomad: a member of a tribe or people having no permanent home, but roaming about constantly in search of food and shelter.

oasis: special areas in a desert which have small reservoirs of water, which then allow the growth of trees and other plants.

obsidian: a type of gemstone which is hard and usually dark in color.

oracle: any person who is believed to be capable of speaking to or communicating with the gods.

pagan: a person who does not have any system of religious belief or worship.

pankus: an assembly of warriors and noblemen during the ancient Hittite rule who helped the king determine political procedure.

papyrus: a type of parchment or paper made from a plant which grew along the Nile River during the time of the ancient Egyptians.

peninsula: a piece of land surrounded by water on all sides, except for a narrow strip which connects it to the mainland.

plateau: an elevated and more or less level expanse of land.

polytheism: belief in the existence of more than one god, or many gods.

portico: a porch or covered walkway.

precipitation: water droplets which are condensed in the earth's atmosphere to form rain, sleet, and snow.

primitive: of or existing in the beginning or earliest times; ancient.

prologue: an introduction; the first part or portion of a literary work, used as preparation for what will follow.

ritual: a system of ceremonies or procedures, especially with regard to religious worship.

sanctuary: a place of peace or safety; a haven or place of rest; a special building set aside for holy worship.

Sanskrit: the ancient, formal language of old India, begun in the fourth century B.C. and still used by Buddhists today.

satraps: the rulers or protectors of individual provinces in ancient Persia.

scribe: a professional writer, manuscript copier, or keeper of written records.

scythe: a long, curved blade set into a handle used to cut grass or grain.

Semitic: an adjective used to connote both languages and populations. Semitic languages are mainly from the Middle East. Semitic populations include the descendants of Sem, a son of Noah.

species: a specific type or class of plant or animal. Plant and animal species are usually very similar and can therefore interbreed only among themselves.

steppe: any of the great plains of Southeast Europe and Asia, having few trees.

sterile: unable to reproduce; barren.

subjugate: to conquer and force into servitude or slavery.

subterranean: living or existing below the surface of the earth.

terrace: a raised, flat mound of earth with sloping sides.

theocracy: a type of government in which the church has priority over and rules the state.

tributary: a small river or stream which usually flows into and is eventually part of a large one.

urban: having to do with the city or city life.

valley: a space of low land wedged between hills or mountains that usually has a stream flowing through it.

vassal: a servant or slave.

ziggurat: multilevel towers used as sanctuaries by the Sumerian empire.

INDEX